D0006198

PITT SERIES IN
NATURE AND NATURAL HISTORY

RATTLER TALES

from Northcentral Pennsylvania

C. E. Brennan

University of Pittsburgh Press
Pittsburgh and London

Published by the University of Pittsburgh Press, Pittsburgh, Pa. 15260
Copyright © 1995, University of Pittsburgh Press
All rights reserved
Manufactured in the United States of America
Printed on acid-free paper
A CIP catalogue record for this book is available from the British Library.
Eurospan, London

Library of Congress Cataloging-in-Publication Data

Brennan, C. E., 1952–
    Rattler tales from northcentral Pennsylvania / C. E. Brennan.
        p.   cm.—(Pitt series in nature and natural history)
    Includes bibliographical references.
    ISBN 0-8229-3856-1.—ISBN 0-8229-5539-3 (pbk.)
    1. Rattlesnake hunting—Pennsylvania.   2. Timber rattlesnake—
Pennsylvania.   3. Brennan, C. E., 1952–   . I. Title.
II. Series.
SK341.S5B74   1994
639'.146' 09748—dc20   94-30898
                                                                    CIP

IN MEMORY OF

Donald N. Williams

DEDICATED TO

Donna, Shanny, and Adam

CONTENTS

FOREWORD

Clark N. Shiffer

DURING MY TEEN YEARS IN THE MID-1950S, IN still largely rural Perry County, Pennsylvania, the hunting and killing of rattlesnakes was very popular. It was not uncommon then to read articles in the local newspapers about successful rattlesnake hunters, often accompanied by photographs showing them hoisting the thick-bodied carcasses of their quarry for all to see. One hunter even sported two well-stocked cartridge belts crisscrossed in true "bandito" style across his chest.

While I did not routinely hunt rattlesnakes then, I viewed them not so much as something to be hated, but as something to be hunted. I particularly remember one early rattlesnake hunt with my brother and a friend. We were all armed—my brother and our friend with shotguns and me with my trusty .22 rifle. We definitely intended to kill any rattlesnakes we saw and at least sever the end of the tail, with its string of rattles, from each carcass.

As we worked our way toward the top of a ridge across the river from town, the electrifying "buzz" of a frightened rattlesnake erupted from the dead leaves close to my brother's feet. I remember his flat-topped hair sticking straight up as he and our friend quickly retreated a short distance downslope. I then shot once, but didn't hit the snake. Almost immediately, my brother wheeled and unloaded a shotgun blast that moved both the still-rattling snake and dead leaves at least three feet from where they had been. Cautiously, we approached the slowly writhing carcass, and when it seemed obvious the snake was dead, I placed my boot on the carcass just behind the head and carefully cut off the head with my pocket knife. I then removed my boot from the carcass and grasped the tail to remove the tip with its rattles. Suddenly, the bloody, decapitated front end swung quickly backward, striking my arm near the wrist. I let out a scream, let go of the tail and jumped away. I'm not sure what my brother and his friend did at that moment, but I don't think they laughed. Regaining my composure, I again placed my boot on the carcass's front end and successfully severed the end of the tail and its rattle string.

Later, after a pause for some lively discussion of this event, we again worked our way toward the top of the ridge, leaving the carcass behind. I took a position slightly to the rear as we threaded our way upslope among the large rocks and, looking at the string of rattles I had removed from my pocket, I thought about the rapid movement of the snake's tail that was required to produce that distinctive buzzing sound. I wondered if I could possibly duplicate the sound by shaking the rattles, held between my thumb and finger, as rapidly as possible. While the resulting sound was only reminiscent of the real thing, it was enough to elicit an immediate response from my brother and our friend. I found myself staring into the muzzles of two shotguns. Following the tersely-worded advice of my brother, I hastily put the rattle string back in my pocket. It stayed there until we left the ridge later, having seen no other rattlesnakes.

Occasionally, during those years, rattlesnake carcasses, minus heads and rattles, were deposited anonymously on our front porch. It was generally known that I was interested in such things, and I marveled at their color patterns and girth. I never seriously considered doing anything with the hides, since my mother always encouraged me to dispose of these unsolicited carcasses as soon as I could.

My interest in snakes, among many other aspects of natural history, continued to grow, and I began to capture and keep nonvenomous snakes. My brother and I and some of our friends would capture black rat snakes and release them in our dirt basement to help control the norway rats that made burrows there. For some time, my mother wondered where all the black snakes were coming from that she would encounter in the backyard, and which she would promptly dispatch with the garden hoe. We couldn't tell her for many years that we had "stocked" them for rodent control. And then there was the smooth green snake that my sister found crawling up her electric blanket cord nearly a year after it escaped from its cage on the front porch. I also remember the black rat snake, longer than I was tall, that I proudly, and somewhat righteously, thrashed to death because it was about to eat some nestling birds. It might have been one of the "stocked" ones that escaped my mother's hoe, only to meet death at the hand of an ignorant teenager who valued its services as a rodent exterminator, but who would deny it another natural food item that was held in higher esteem than the rodent.

My teenage ambivalence toward snakes was a reflection of the larger community attitudes about snakes prevalent in the fifties. A *National Geographic* article in 1954, entitled "Our Snake Friends and Foes," by Doris M. Cochran, caught my eye, both for the wonderful illustrations by Walter A. Weber and the information it contained. Here was an authoritative article written in popular style by an associate curator of the Division of Reptiles and Amphibians at the U.S. National Museum. (I clipped the article from the magazine and still have it.) The general tone of the article was that, most of the time, snakes are beneficial and, indeed, our friends. But, as the title says, they are sometimes our foes, meaning that they can be "prejudicial (tending to injure or impair) or injurious," as Webster defines the word. The venomous snakes would qualify as foes when humans are (very rarely) bitten and poisoned by them.

Near the end of the article Cochran responds to inquiries about how to exterminate rattlesnakes near mountain camps or homes by saying that "perhaps the most effective way is to dynamite the hibernating dens during the winter season when the snakes are inside." For a variety of reasons, this practice was not carried out in any serious, sustained, or widespread way, although the dynamiting of rattlesnake habitat as a means of exterminating rattlesnakes is a matter of record. Not the least of the reasons dynamiting of dens, or *hibernacula,* has not been widespread, much less effective, is that they are not easily located. Probably more dens have been destroyed inadvertently by dynamiting during construction projects in mountainous terrain than have been blown up by design. The author partially redeems herself when, near the very end of the article, she says, "in unpopulated areas even the poisonous snakes can be beneficial."

In 1955 the Morris Township Volunteer Fire Company, in the village of Morris, Tioga County, Pennsylvania, began a rattlesnake roundup. It bills itself as affiliated with the International Association of Rattlesnake Hunters, headquartered in Okeene, Oklahoma. It is the oldest such event in Pennsylvania, continuing to the present, although it is now become something of an added attraction alongside a major softball tournament held during the second weekend in June.

I first became directly acquainted with the Morris Rattlesnake Hunt and other organized snake hunts in 1977, one year after becoming the herpetology and endangered species coordinator with what was then called the Pennsylvania Fish Commission (now the Pennsylvania Fish and Boat Commission). Curt Brennan recounts briefly our first contact shortly thereafter in the pages that follow. I had been employed by the commission for ten years, doing lake and stream management work as a fisheries biologist. The chance to become reacquainted with "nongame" fishes, amphibians, reptiles, and aquatic organisms of many kinds, including "species of special concern," was exciting and challenging.

Shortly after passage of the federal Endangered Species Act of 1973, and some prodding from the U.S. Fish and Wildlife Service, the recently appointed executive director of the Fish

Commission, Ralph W. Abele, sought and received from the state legislature in 1974 official jurisdiction for all commonwealth amphibians, reptiles, and aquatic organisms, including those to be classified as endangered and threatened. Within two more years, the first application form and permit governing the conduct of organized snake hunts was drawn up by the administrative offices in Harrisburg. In 1977 the executive director appointed members of a herpetology advisory committee to assist the commission with its new role to officially protect, conserve, and enhance the amphibian and reptile fauna of the state.

At that time there were seven permitted organized snake hunts, including the one at Morris. The others were held in Sinnemahoning, Cameron County (one by the Keystone Reptile Club, Inc., and another by the Sinnemahoning Sportsmen's Club); in Noxen, Wyoming County (Keystone Reptile Club); in Landisburg, Perry County (Keystone Reptile Club); in Cross Fork, Potter County (Kettle Creek Hose Company); and at Indian Steps Museum near Airville, York County (Conservation Society of York County). The last was mostly a copperhead hunt; the others mostly timber rattlesnake hunts. Between 1977 and 1993 at least ten other hunts were held and discontinued. The York County Hunt was terminated in 1993 by action of the society, having been the second oldest such event in the state. Discounting the York County Hunt, eleven organized hunts received permits in 1993, a large number of them conducted as fund raising events for rural fire companies and sportsmen's organizations, by the Keystone Reptile Club and the Mon-River Reptile Association.

All Keystone Reptile Club and Mon-River Reptile Association hunts feature, at the end of the two to four day event, "sacking" contests, where two-person teams, men and/or women, compete against the clock in placing five live rattlesnakes in a sack or cloth bag, one at a time. One team member is the handler and picks up the snakes from the floor of an elevated, fenced platform, while the partner holds and maneuvers the bag. Teams are disqualified if a member is bitten by a snake or a snake is judged to be seriously injured. A similar event with nonvenomous snakes for women and children takes place at Keystone Club events. Contest winners get trophies and public recognition for their "feats."

In 1984 it became illegal to use snakes captured in Pennsylvania (venomous or nonvenomous) in sacking contests. However, it is still legal to import snakes from other states for sacking, with the exception of the timber rattlesnake. Legally imported Western diamondback rattlesnakes are now used for sacking. Sacking by women and children also continues, using nonvenomous snakes said to come from other states, and therefore not under the protection of the Fish and Boat Commission, but which may have been collected illegally in Pennsylvania. A proposal to ban the importation of all Pennsylvania snakes for sacking in the 1993 Fish and Boat Commission regulations governing the conduct of organized snake hunts was not implemented as a result of political pressure.

Why is snake sacking such an important issue? Because its negative educational impact is so great, and it does not contribute to the protection, conservation, or enhancement of this Pennsylvania resource. Similar displays using other small animals would simply not be tolerated. Most important, this treatment of snakes reinforces the negative feelings many people already have about these animals. If snakes of any kind, venomous or not, are ever to be accepted for what they *really* are and given respect for their natural roles, we need to take responsibility for positive education on their behalf, rather than continuing to sacrifice them on the altars of political expediency, popularity, or ignorance.

A legal technicality will continue to allow the sacking of imported snakes in Pennsylvania unless there is a ban on importation, perhaps also by other states. Until then the carnival spectacle, which hunt organizers condone as necessary for drawing crowds and raising money, will go on to the continued detriment of the nation's snake population. The fact that there are very successful organized snake hunts in Pennsylvania that have never sacked snakes makes a lie of the contention that sacking contests are necessary.

Although Curt Brennan discusses organized snake hunts, I believe it is important that readers know something more about this aspect of his story. Sadly, the general public is as hostile to snakes as it was in the 1950s, especially toward venomous snakes, or those believed to be venomous. The vast majority of people still cannot confidently distinguish venomous and nonvenomous snakes and don't seem to know where such information can be found. Although almost everyone calling the Fish and Boat Commission to report seeing or killing a snake claims that it was a copperhead, subsequent examinations reveal that all but a very few are nonvenomous.

Read carefully the story that unfolds in the following pages. Let it acquaint you with an animal that will need more of our help in the future, so that it and the wildness it represents are not lost to us and those that follow. Learn something about those who pursue timber rattlesnakes, and why. Allow the story to make you laugh, and then cause you to think seriously. When you have finished, you may want to read all or some of it again. You may come to realize, as I did, that although this story has an end, it is far from over. Some who read this are already helping to write future chapters of *Rattler Tales*.

PREFACE

I T IS NO SECRET THAT WITHIN THE SECTION OF PENN-
sylvania's Appalachian Mountains called the Mountainous
High Plateau one can still experience nature as it was known to
the hunters and woodsmen of the past. Here was the campsite of
"Nessmuk," the trapline of E. N. Woodcock, and the Black Forest of Henry Shoemaker's mountain stories.* It is a rugged portion of Northcentral Pennsylvania that remains unfit for the
plow, hostile toward road builders, and hard on lumbermen. It
is a contiguous stretch of hardwood forest regenerated from the
ashes of widespread fires that followed the logging of virgin
conifers around the turn of the century. The heart of this section is largely state forest lands, an annual staging area for deer,
bear, and turkey hunters who call it the Big Woods.

In his book *Thirty Years a Hunter,* published in 1854, the pioneer Philip Tome provided us with colorful descriptions of the
wolves, elk, and panthers he encountered in the mountains of
Northcentral Pennsylvania. With the taming of the wilderness,
that trio of mammals vacated the premises. The timber rattlesnake, the only other wild creature that truly excited Tome, still
remains in the Big Woods, although over the years a multitude
of folks have tried their best to exterminate the species. I helped
them for a while; now, I want to make restitution.

I've hunted timber rattlers in Northcentral Pennsylvania for
twenty years. For the past fifteen, I've referred to my passion as

---

*"Nessmuk" was the pen name of George W. Sears, a Tioga County resident,
camper, and canoe enthusiast of the late 1800s. His book *Woodcraft* was originally
published in 1923. Woodcock, author of *Fifty Years a Hunter* was born in Lymans-
ville, Potter County, in 1844. Shoemaker published *Black Forest Souvenirs* in 1914.

"rattlesnake observing"; I take a few snakes, but only for what I consider useful purposes (which doesn't include hatbands or fang necklaces). The snake has suffered a noticeable, rapid decline in recent years. When I plot the locations of denning areas that my comrades and I locate, I have visions of someday turning the maps over to the biologist charged with locating the last pair of timber rattlers on Earth. I hope it doesn't come to that, but we humans are quite talented at forcing other species to the brink of extinction. I want to give the timber rattlesnake a break by intercepting the new generation of rattlesnake hunters before they recklessly deliver the final blow.

In order to dispel the myths that surround the timber rattlesnake and help you discover what a fascinating creature it is, I present highlights of its natural history in the chapters that follow. This is a blend of currently available literature, my own observations, and the observations of those whom I consider to be reliable sources. Some of the information is speculation—it remains to be substantiated or disproved by specific, reputable scientific studies. Howard K. Reinert, one of Pennsylvania's

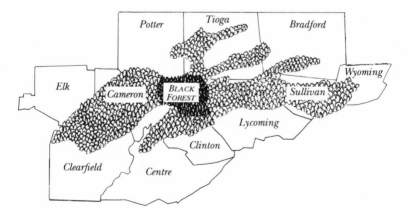

THE COUNTIES OF NORTHCENTRAL PENNSYLVANIA
(THE MOUNTAINOUS HIGH PLATEAU) SHOWING THE LOCATION
OF THE BIG WOODS.

leading snake ecologists, has made notable discoveries through his extensive timber rattlesnake research during the past fifteen years, some of which are mentioned herein.

I contemplated whether or not to provide instruction on capturing timber rattlesnakes, since my intention is to prevent further erosion of its existing population. A friend (who, in part, made this publication possible) argued that I should delete the related chapter. But people will continue to kill or collect timber rattlers in Pennsylvania. Someone is always available to demonstrate unnecessary and extreme techniques for "handling" rattlers. A rock, skidding tire, firearm, shovel, clamp, or noose, stands between its user and the opportunity to understand the true nature of the snake. I believe that, if this reptile is to survive, some of the mystery surrounding it must be removed. And it's time to dim the fallacious aura of challenge in pursuing a timber rattler. It hurts when I learn of yet another "young buck" who conquered a rattler and brought its mutilated carcass back for public display; and it sickens me to hear of a mature woodsman doing exactly the same.

We should not attack the snakes, but the fear of the unknown that is responsible for the demise of so many nonthreatening timber rattlers. And the rattlesnake exhibitionists, those who perpetuate the myth of the evil and menacing snake, must be sent on to new challenges that require true grit. Thus, the reader is warned that this account of my experiences, and those of my partners and the fellow snake hunters I interviewed, is not supposed to frighten or sensationalize, but is intended to portray our evolution from snake takers to snake observers.

The path of the timber rattlesnake leads to sparkling mountain brooks and sphagnum bogs, through dense thickets of mountain laurel and sweet fern, and beneath tightly woven canopies of hemlock and white pine. It leads to pinnacles of weather-beaten sandstones and across carpets of shalerock. It is a path of no end, circling wildly in the heart of the Black Forest. It begs to be trod upon, so long as it is treated with care and respect. It leads through an endless mass of sights, sounds, feelings, and aromas more addictive than the most notorious of narcotics.

Rattler Tales is a snake hunter's account of the timber rattlesnake in Pennsylvania's Big Woods and Black Forest country. It profiles the snake, the actions of people who live in its territory, and, humorously at times, the men who pursue it. The book answers the most commonly asked questions about the timber rattler, and it squelches sage-old myths. It offers safety suggestions for those entering rattler woods and describes the restraints necessary if the species is to survive.

I wish to thank the following cooperators who played major roles in formulating *Rattler Tales:*

Tushanna Brennan, Becky Wilber, and Catherine Kittle, patient and diligent typists;

Betty Malloy, Marcia Bonta, and Catherine Marshall for their editing and moral support;

Allan Puskar, who provided information through the years and reviewed the manuscript for technical accuracy;

Howard K. Reinert, who sent his research reports, shared additional current findings, and reviewed "They Have a Friend in Pennsylvania";

Clark Shiffer, who provided information, a technical review, and support;

John H. Way, who helped me to form a geological description of Northcentral den rocks.

My comrades afield and the other subjects mentioned herein, who are truly "the stuff" of *Rattler Tales.*

RATTLER TALES FROM
NORTHCENTRAL PENNSYLVANIA

1

Birth of a Snake Hunter

THIRTY-TWO YEARS AGO I STOOD ON THE FACE OF
Little Pine Dam in Lycoming County, Pennsylvania, watching my cousins and the other older kids fling stones at a
rattlesnake. I could clearly hear the snake "buzzing," but I was
forbidden to get close enough to see it. When the kids were
finished, there was a heap of rocks the size of a kitchen range in
the vicinity of the rattler's last known "buzz." I was a bit excited
and somewhat frightened, but I secretly hoped that the snake
had escaped unharmed.

I was intrigued by timber rattlesnakes as far back as I can
remember. I looked forward to Sunday afternoons during the
summers when Dad would say, "Let's go for a ride." Leaving
Williamsport, we'd head north, then travel on forest roads to
places like Masten, Rock Run, Leetonia, or Slate Run. In those
days, it was fairly common to encounter an awkwardly parked
vehicle with its doors ajar. Its passengers were usually nearby,
"polishing off" a timber rattler they had run over on the road or
spotted in the ditch. I always wished that we would find our own
rattler on the road so I could get a better look at the mystical
creature I'd heard so much about. We also made several trips to
the Morris Rattlesnake Hunt, then in its heyday. I was overwhelmed by the sights and sounds and hoped that someday I
could join the circle of nimrods who captured the rattlers.

Trying to recall the details of my high school days is often an
exercise in futility, but I do remember a personal adventure
recounted by Lewis "Lewy" McKeague, my sophomore history

teacher. I cannot remember if the prelude concerned rattlesnakes, fishing, or how an individual reacts to fear; I came to attention when I heard "rattlesnake." Lewy told us that he had been fly-fishing one evening on Rock Run. (The lower end of the creek tumbles through a glen for a mile or so, to its confluence with Lycoming Creek. Once you start up through the glen, there are only a few places where you can safely climb back up to the road, which parallels the stream.) After fishing his way into the glen and picking up a few trout, Lewy decided to call it a day. He broke down his rod and started climbing the rock face that formed one side of the hole he had been fishing. After climbing vertically about ten feet above the deep pool, he came eye-to-eye with a timber rattler. Lewy exclaimed to the class, "I was never a good diver, but let me tell you! I did a beautiful back flip—hip boots, creel, net, rod, hat, and all—into the pool below!"

I was trout fishing on Blockhouse Creek with my father when I experienced my first solo encounter with a timber rattlesnake. As I fished a deep riffle, I noticed a hunk of wood drifting down toward me. I thought it peculiar that the branch was crossing the creek faster than it was drifting. The stick, a large black rattler, crawled onto the small gravel bar where I stood. I held motionless as it gracefully eased past me and into the grass. "Wow!" I thought. "I wonder if I can ketch 'im!" I quickly formed a loop of fly line at the tip of my rod (the old "loop at the end of a stick" trick) and placed it over the snake's head. I carefully snugged the line and lifted. My fly rod doubled and the snake's head rose, but I couldn't begin to raise its body with such flimsy gear. The snake remained placid and unimpressed by my feeble attempt to curtail its journey. I called for Dad, who was a short distance downstream and around the bend. I wanted him to see the snake—perhaps decide if we should do anything with it. (Dad was quick to behead copperheads in the vicinity of our home.) When Dad sized up the situation, he advised, "Best leave him alone. He's not going to bother anyone way out here."

In the spring of 1973 I was introduced firsthand to the sport of rattlesnake hunting by the forest ranger Ray Low, a slim and elusive ridgerunner from Leetonia. I had begun employment with the Pennsylvania Bureau of Forestry the previous summer and, from the start, I heard numerous tales about Ray and his rattlesnakes. He is a true Leetonian, born and reared near the ghost lumber town on the headwaters of Cedar Run. Although he only attended school through the eighth grade and claims "they didn't teach me nothing," when it comes to navigating the forest, bagging bucks and gobblers, keeping bees, trapping coons, catching the big browns, and cutting timber, Ray outshines the best of them; and a more congenial man would be a saint. He took me snaking a few times that spring, and I watched him catch a dozen or more rattlers. I studied the habitat and later began referring to good rattlesnake rocks as "Ray Low rocks." I dubbed his short and slender style of snake stick the "Ray Low stick." During the twenty years that followed, the best denning areas I located were in Ray Low rocks. The best all-around snake stick is the Ray Low stick. Knowing Ray's credentials, I was foolish to try and make any new discoveries or improvements.

I knew, minutes into the first excursion with Ray, that I was hooked on timber rattlesnake hunting. This was something I had to learn more about, and I began pursuing my new-found hobby with a signal passion. In June I was going out alone, hunting the ridges near Ansonia. I had heard an announcement on the local radio station that rattlesnake hunters were welcome on the Confer farm. I found my first rattler in a small shalerock outcropping about a hundred yards behind their pasture. The snake was ready to shed and had a strange blue cast to its color, the likes of which I have never seen since. After fumbling for some time, I managed to get the lively serpent into my sack. I suppose I would have been quite a sight, had someone witnessed that first attempt of mine to bag a rattler. The two infant snakes that lay nearby were spared, as I feared they would slip through the tears in the crusty burlap sack.

The following spring I began searching for rattlesnakes early, probably weeks before their normal emergence date. I noticed that the garter snakes were up and about; therefore, I figured, the rattlers would also be "awake." I went up Asaph Run and found a nice looking rock pile. There weren't any rattlers in sight, so I began flipping rocks. Still no snakes, so I dug through another layer. Soon I had to stop and move the large slag pile I was creating, in order to make standing room. After excavating a couple of feet into the outcropping, I found the lifeless form of a twenty-one-inch serpent that appeared to be a timber rattler. I surmised that it wasn't rattling because there was ice inside its rattle. I hauled my prized catch off the ridge and stopped to show Elwood Wilson in Asaph. Elwood laughed and shook his head when I dumped the rigid snake out of the sack. "The dang thing's still froze," he giggled.

A month later, when the rattlers had finally surfaced, I headed for the hill where I had captured the blue rattler. Returning to the same outcropping, I found nothing except the uprooted mess of rocks I had left the previous year. Even the small snakes must have abandoned the site. I trudged up the steep point, zigzagging from ledge to ledge, trying to find a snake. I had worked my way to the top ledges at the rim of the mountain when a movement to my right caught my attention. A somewhat short, sleek, and muscular life form was dashing from ledge to ledge, picking and rooting like a wild boar. It was another snake hunter! He was clutching a small white sack in one hand and methodically working an aluminum snake pincer with the other. He was hatless and wore only a thin T-shirt as if immune to the baneful blackflies; and he wore low-cut carpenter shoes as if there were no rattlesnakes. His greased, sandy hair was neatly swept back as though the year were 1955; his deeply tanned and weather-beaten face blended with the shalerock background. He seemed surprised when he looked toward the next pile of suspect snake rocks and noticed me standing on them. "What are you doing here?" he asked, in a manner revealing that he *knew* what I was doing there. Before I could reply, he added, "I've hunted snakes for a long time and this is the first time I ran into another hunter." He was the legendary rattlesnake hunter John Howe, of Lawrenceville. He opened his snake bag, displaying a plump, three-foot yellow rattler he had sacked several minutes earlier. We began to root through the rocks together. "You know, there aren't many snakes around anymore," he said. "Too many guys haul rock," he grunted as he flipped a piece of shalerock the size of a desk top. "Each time we come through and do this, the rocks wind up farther and farther down the mountain."

At sunset that evening, John rolled into our driveway in an old Ford Galaxy, trunk lid flopping in the breeze. A plywood box, now laden with timber rattlers, had been closely fitted to the walls of the trunk. I called for Donna, my wife, to come see. John raised the box's lid and, with his pincers, withdrew a large yellow specimen. He swiftly pinned the snake and held it up in his true, photogenic style—having had considerable practice at the annual trophy presentation ceremonies at the Morris Rattlesnake Hunt.

2

There Were No Rules

ARLY IN 1975 I WAS FORTUNATE TO GAIN A valuable snake hunting partner for years to come. Gary Dillman, an ardent outdoorsman, was working out of our forestry headquarters in Wellsboro at the time. He was interested in my snake-hunting tales and, although an avid fly-fisherman, decided to lay the rod aside one evening to accompany me. As in my case, Gary was quickly hooked, and we embarked on a ruthless quest to win a trophy at the Morris Rattlesnake Hunt as soon as possible.

Throughout the late spring and early summer of 1975, Gary and I hunted timber rattlers at a feverish pace. We were still novices: studying the habitat, learning the relationship of weather to snake sightings, scouring ridge upon ridge to locate denning areas, and practicing various techniques for handling the rattlers. Evenings and weekends found us racing up and down rocky, laurel-choked inclines so steep that even the wood rats avoided them.

We weren't accumulating enough snakes to win anything at Morris, and we didn't want to sell them to buyers or kill them for the one dollar bounty. It seemed like everyone we knew wanted a rattler for one reason or another, and we wound up giving many away. They went for display cases, stew, hatbands, belts, and mounts. The remaining snakes we had hauled in were inadvertently used for ineffectual restocking attempts, the timber rattler being a far more complex animal than we had imagined.

Our ruthless methods of handling the snakes and tearing up their favorite haunts were severely damaging both the animals and our chances of ever winning a trophy. We began to wonder if we were doing the proper thing. We weren't breaking any laws because there were none; there was a bounty on the rattlers, so they must be evil.

In May 1976 Gary and I checked some of the dens we had pilfered during the prior season. Upon finding very few snakes and a lot of damaged cover, just as we had left it, we began to realize we would have to drastically alter our hunting methods if we intended to perpetuate the sport. Not being fully convinced or willing to change completely, we pressed on, with minor modifications. We decided we would only displace rocks that harbored snakes for certain, and we would return the rocks to their original positions, if possible.

On most of the hills where we hunted we found evidence of past rattler hunting. The face of a surface rock, exposed to the elements for years on end, has a shade and texture that is quite distinguishable from its underside. It was obvious that many of the talus slopes had been raked viciously by previous hunters. Based on material and vegetative conditions under and surrounding the discolored rocks, we determined that some of the slides had been worked over repeatedly through the years. In areas like these, we found it difficult to locate even one or two timber rattlesnakes. If we wanted larger numbers of snakes, we would have to go deeper into the woods and find some "virgin" den sites.

On a fair evening in early June, Gary and I headed deep into the North Block of the Tioga State Forest, for we had heard that a logging crew was running into an unusually abundant supply of rattlers in one section. Upon reaching the scene, we thoroughly inspected the rocky sidehill adjacent to the log job and found one small snake. At the point of the ridge, we debated crossing a steep ravine to hunt the adjacent mountainside—we were calculating the remaining daylight in minutes. Trudging onward, we crossed the gully and began picking through a steep acreage of ledges and rubble.

Nearing the end of the ledges and noticing a likely spot below us, we dropped downslope and entered the nicest piece of virgin shalerock we had ever seen. In the upper quadrant lay a three-foot-square chunk of stone that had "rattlesnake hotel" written all over it. A telltale yellow loop protruding from the lower side strengthened our belief that we had discovered Jackpot Rock. We strung our snake bags in a nearby birch in anticipation of a good catch and carefully positioned our snake sticks on the big slab for a smooth and rapid joint haul. When we made the flip, there were snakes scurrying in all directions. By the time we finished bagging them—twenty-one in all—and checking the surrounding rocks, it was dark. Sacks in hand, we stumbled and picked our way along the steep hillside and across the ravine. Had the sacks contained medical supplies for a disaster-stricken village, we probably would have dropped them; but these were our very own live timber rattlers.

Within two weeks, knowing we didn't have enough snakes to win at Morris, we carried the rattlers, including ones from other locations, back to Jackpot Rock. We spent some time tidying the place up a bit prior to making the release. (Using our bare hands to restore the appearance of the rattlesnake den was a little nerve-racking, especially since we suspected that we didn't notice all the inhabitants on our first visit.)

I believe that Jackpot would have survived its rude upset if the story had ended with our gallant restoration effort. On the contrary, later that summer, in an egotistical display to prove my worthiness as a ridgerunner, I guided a misfit troop of conservation corps youths to the very location. The trip was to be an environmental education experience—certainly a worthy cause—and the youngsters would never know where they were or tell anyone. Wrong! One of the boys knew exactly where he was, and his dad worked with a fellow who had a reputation for being downright hard on rattlesnakes.

When Gary and I returned to Jackpot Rock early in the 1977 season, it looked like a large bulldozer had been on the scene. There wasn't an unturned rock. The rattlers were gone—and I was solely to blame. I had committed the ultimate crime against my partner.

Several days later, after Gary forgave me (I think he did), we decided that the time was right. We had tucked away some reserve hot spots, and we decided to cash in and head for Morris. During the following three weeks we pounded the turf, high and low, far and wide, stockpiling our snakes—three from one

ridge, nine from another. On the day of the Morris Hunt, we spent the early afternoon transferring the rattlers from our wooden storage box into field sacks in order to make our entry at the pit look authentic. We packaged the snakes by size to prevent crushing the smaller ones. At 3:31:15 P.M. we donned clean clothing, washed our faces in a nearby brook, and combed our hair neatly in preparation for the trophy presentation ceremony and photo session. With everything in order, we were off to Morris.

The rules at the annual Morris Rattlesnake Hunt, as far as we knew, were: "There are no rules." Whoever paid the two-dollar registration fee and entered the pit with live timber rattlers prior to 5:00 P.M. on Hunt Saturday was eligible to win any of several or more trophies: "Longest," "Most," "Most Rattles," and so on. "Most" could be by a two-man team. No questions were asked concerning how, when, or where you acquired your rattlers; and there was no honor among competing rattlesnake hunters. The hard-core competitors tried to hold out until the last few minutes. If they thought someone were going to outdo them, they would not enter their snakes. (At the time, the hunt sponsor kept all entries. Some hunters would return the unentered snakes to the den, sell them to a buyer, or enter them at another snake hunt.)

Gary and I wheeled into Morris at 4:45 and, bags of snakes in hand, walked toward the pit. The area was encompassed by a dense wall of onlookers, as regular winners John Howe and Gary Wier were inside unveiling their take. Gary and I slowly made our way through the first layers of the crowd and hung back, just out of sight of Howe, Wier, and the pit officials. We held our bags low and tried to stifle the reactions of people whose legs we were brushing with our bags of rattlers. Ray Low, Jimm Leach, and Rawley Grant, wanting to see us win, moved in around us to afford more camouflage and to offer their snakes if necessary. (Of course, Gary and I were the only two honorable rattlesnake hunters to ever hit the circuit; we didn't really want to cheat.) Howe had the "Longest" sewn up at fifty inches, easily beating our forty-six-incher.

At 4:55, Amos Osborn, a pit official, had finished counting. He looked at Howe and Wier and asked, "Is that it?" They nodded, and Amos announced that the duo had taken the lead with fifty-five snakes. Gary and I moved to the entrance gate and got Amos's attention. He flagged us in. John Howe's eyes lit up like a pine stump on a night fire. Gary Wier reached behind and picked up another bag or two of snakes and hollered at Amos, who shook his head. No—there was a rule!

Laughter and jeers, mostly from our friends, erupted from the crowd as Gary and I dumped the first bag of sized snakes, the smallest. Amos scurried to put the tiny critters into the inner pit before they escaped through the outer mesh holding the spectators at bay. The oohs and aahs of the audience intensified as we dumped the bags of larger snakes. We knew exactly how many rattlers we had—sixty-seven—but you don't argue with officials, so we had to settle for their count of seventy. We had our trophy.

Gary and I knew we would never enter timber rattlesnakes in a quantity contest again. We enjoyed the hunting more than the taking. Down deep, I wasn't a bit proud and felt that I had sold out on the rattlers and my favorite hobby. The only consolation was in hoping that maybe someday someone with the authority to protect the rattlers would listen to the concerns of a converted rattlesnake killer. A year or so earlier I had asked a Tioga County commissioner what procedure could be used to lift the venerable bounty. "I don't know of anyone that wants it lifted!" he snapped without further discussion. (Did that mean he didn't know me, or did that mean I was a nobody?)

During the years following the 1977 hunt, Gary and I began our own small campaign, trying to reduce peoples' unwarranted fear of timber rattlers and attempting to draw attention to the snakes' impending extirpation locally. I wrote the Pennsylvania Fish Commission (now the Pennsylvania Fish and Boat Commission), which is charged with managing the commonwealth's reptiles and amphibians. At the time, it was kicking around some prospective rattlesnake legislation. I received a decent and favorable reply, and its herpetology and endangered species co-ordinator, Clark Shiffer, contacted Gary and me. Clark accompanied us on a hunt and seemed to have a feel for the sport, including a thorough understanding of the rattlesnake's potential doom if uncontrolled exploitation were to continue. He taught us a good deal, relating various bits of information he had acquired on timber rattlesnake behavior and status.

In 1980 Gary and I submitted an article to the *Wellsboro Gazette* expressing our concern that the timber rattler population might be declining at an alarming rate. The *Gazette* ran the article with the headline "We Have a 'No Kill' Policy on Rattlesnakes," along with a photo Gary took of me standing next to a snake. They placed it adjacent to an article about that year's Morris Rattlesnake Hunt. (The next several times I was in Morris, I ducked.) John Howe thought Gary and I had formulated a hoax and were stockpiling thousands of snakes to set an all-time record at Morris. We used to stop at the hunt each year in an effort to terrorize him. He would always ask us where we were hiding our snakes.

Gary and I continued to hunt snakes, capturing only an occasional specimen for educational purposes. Gary became involved in preparing environmental displays, presenting timber rattler programs, and handling "nuisance" rattlers at the Tioga-Hammond Dam park complex where he works. I had the honor of conducting some visitor programs at Leonard Harrison and Hills Creek State Park environmental centers, and I met with Wilderness Experience and Youth Conservation Corps groups for several years.

Allan Puskar, a Wellsboro High School ecology teacher, began displaying an arrant interest in protecting the timber rattlesnake after hunting with Gary and me on several occasions and learning of the snake's status. He began studying various aspects of timber rattler behavior and amassed previously published scientific information. Al assembled an excellent lecture-slide program and made presentations to various groups, while simultaneously pleading with the public and officials to stifle the unchecked destruction of the timber rattlesnake and its habitat.

The wheels in Harrisburg were already churning, and, perhaps in our more environmentally indoctrinated times, some mandated protection for the timber rattler was inevitable. I like to believe that we converted rattlesnake killers had a hand in seeing it through. Much work remains—before it's too late for "old velvet tail."

3

Living with Rattlers

SCATTERED THROUGHOUT NORTHCENTRAL PENNSYL-vania are insular hamlets tucked in the narrow valleys carved by the West Branch headwaters—places like Forksville, Marsh Hill, English Center, and Cammal. Many of the communities have formed TV associations. Each association erects a small tower on top of the neighboring ridge, strings a cable, and builds a small shack to house the necessary electronic paraphernalia.

Inevitably, a porcupine wanders to the site, chews a hole through the side of the shanty, enters, and gnaws on everything that is crucial to the operation of the system. The resulting outage is normally just prior to prime time on a drizzly Friday evening. Two of the association handymen fire up an old Jeep, throw in a chain saw and toolbox, and head for the mountain.

The journey to the tower site takes about forty-five minutes if there are no hitches. They drive up the highway several miles and turn left on a forestry road so steep that the boulders have a hard time staying in the wheel tracks, then hang a left on a clay-base lane with ruts deep enough to engulf a medium-sized bear.

The townsfolk below, anxious for a report, time the journey and step outdoors when the men are about to reach the tower site. Silence indicates that there will be TV shortly. A barely audible whining echo denotes, "Get out the cards for an hour or two." If the hollering seems a bit profane and is loud enough to trigger a small rook, the patrons know it is porcupine damage and promptly organize a fund-raiser. TV associations hate porcupines.

Seed-corn growers erect electronic scare devices to keep blackbirds away. They hate blackbirds.

The Christmas tree growers use sprays and poison pellets to protect their stock from mice, but during the right kind of a winter the little buggers girdle the trees anyway. They hate mice.

Trout fishermen on Pine Creek hate some of the "trash fish" they catch; they throw them up on the bank "for the 'coons."

But the creature that many of these people and others hate in common is the timber rattlesnake.

When rattlers were plentiful, most of the regular users of the forest roads were experts at killing them. Their weapon was the family car, a truck, or whatever they happened to be driving at the time. Being an expert was having the ability to spot the snake at a distance, increasing acceleration while warning the wife and kids to brace themselves, and slamming the brake pedal at the precise moment to insure a good, hard skid over the rattler's midsection. With experience, an expert didn't have to risk his life collecting the rattles for the kids—the rattles having been smashed or thrown fifty or sixty feet into the woods during the slide. It would take the driver and passengers twenty minutes or so to cool down after such a close encounter with death.

Some of the local rattlesnake hunters don't help the snake's image. They enhance public fear of the snake in order to promote themselves as a rare breed of tough, fearless heroes. The more people they can terrorize with rattlers, the bigger their egos grow. Most people don't realize that the biggest dangers in hunting timber rattlesnakes are dehydration and sprained ankles.

Participants in the pit shows at many of Pennsylvania's rattlesnake roundups also contribute to this disinformation campaign. I suggest that some of the snake handlers never finished a climb on a backwoods ridge or, for that matter, went far enough into the brush that they couldn't look back and see their vehicles.

They wear knee-high leather boots and fancy wide-brimmed hats that a ridgerunner wouldn't be caught dead in. They carry goofy curlicue snake sticks that look like something one would use to clean a crooked sewer pipe. After missing on several pin attempts, they partly crush the snake's head, then, grasping its head and neck with a choke hold tight enough to down a Bengal tiger, they parade it before the spectators' clattering cameras. When his hand starts cramping up, "Mr. Rodeo" drops the snake and waves his stick in front of its nose. After much prodding, the snake strikes, breaking a fang on the "sewer cleaner." Knowing the snake won't hit the steel rod again, the cowboy raises his six-pound boot, forcing another broken fang. Yippee! Let's get a fresh snake and start over!

Even the conservation agencies (fish, game, and forestry) have their share of timber rattlesnake haters. A high-ranking conservation officer was driving by a local natural area shortly after it had been posted against the hunting, capturing, or killing of any reptiles or amphibians. He heard the telltale "buzz" of a rattler coming from the natural area side of the road. He stopped his vehicle, got out, and hunted up a pole (about ten feet long). Realizing the snake was in the natural area, he proceeded to coax it onto the road. Then, everything being legal, he began bashing wildly. A second officer, who was following along behind, stopped to finish the job with a shorter, nine-foot pole.

Any species of snake may be attacked by humans. I had a neighbor who went to great lengths to eradicate the garter snakes on his property. He would stand on watch, like a deer hunter, with his shotgun aimed at the lumber pile. When a snake got up enough courage to try to soak in a little sun, he'd cut loose, splintering boards beyond usability. Then he would sprinkle talcum powder around the woodpile in an effort to track down survivors and detect newcomers. I observed him flailing his hoe frantically in his garden one evening. I thought he had finally found a cluster of spuds that were larger than golf balls. When I looked up again, he was rapidly approaching, hoe in hand. I figured he was coming to show me a potato. When he was in range, I saw the lifeless form of an infant snake draped over the hoe blade. He was certain he "had him" a copperhead. It was a milk snake. If he had spent a little time tidying up his property he wouldn't have had the snake "problem." The junk piles, weeds, and numerous sheds made his place a snake haven.

Even the farmer's friend, the blacksnake, is not spared by the indiscriminate snake killers. They were fairly common in my boyhood community (blacksnakes *and* snake killers). Also common was the shriek of a neighborhood lady—the standard "blacksnake alarm." In a matter of seconds, a gentleman equipped with a long-handled shovel would appear on the scene to dispatch the "ugly culprit."

Dad, his friend Andy, and I went fishing on Schrader Creek one spring day. We arrived at Laquin during mid-morning and began hiking up an old logging road that parallels the creek. Andy took the lead; I was a step behind, to his right. We were pacing along rapidly in anticipation of some good fishing. Suddenly, in one blurred motion, Andy leaped into the air, landed gracefully in a squatting position, grasped a palm-sized rock, righted himself, and fired the rock onto the head of a large, black, coiled snake. The snake, which I hadn't noticed until Andy delivered the lethal blow, was a blacksnake. Andy said, "Hum, thought it was a rattler."

Perhaps we should take a closer look at how ferocious snakes really are, in general. For openers, I would like to refer to the example set by my second-grade classmate, Cindy Larson. Cindy would bring ringneck and garter snakes to school in a lunch box. After some persuasion from the class, our teacher would allow Cindy to let the snakes loose so we could watch her handle them. The snakes would crawl about on her desk and across her arms. Other classmates (the girls were the only ones brave enough) would touch or hold the snakes. When she returned home, Cindy would release the snakes and hunt up a few new ones for the next day. She didn't want to keep them from their home for too long.

Not all snakes are as docile as Cindy's ringnecks, but species native to Northcentral Pennsylvania, given a chance, will run or hide rather than fight. I've heard a few stories to the contrary, but I have yet to see a snake, timber rattlers included, go on the offensive. When a snake strikes to hit something other than dinner, it is a last resort defense tactic. Gary Dillman and I observed, handled, or captured 147 timber rattlers one summer and witnessed not a solitary strike. We approached them without creating a ruckus, picking many of them up gently with non-squeezing snake sticks. In twenty years of hunting timber rattlers, which included hundreds of rambles through rocky and brush-laden denning areas, I was never struck by a snake. I can recall only two instances when rattlers feigned strikes at me when I carelessly stumbled to within inches of them. They could have easily hit home had they so desired. The only time a rattler tried to bite me was when I grabbed one's tail section as it crawled into a crevice. Unbeknown to me, its foresection exited another fissure to the left of my tugging hand. I wondered why my partner was acting so panicky; then I noticed the flickering of a set of high-speed chops about five inches from my wrist and wishing for a little slack. (Given a chance, that snake would have taken the starch out of my love for the pastime; but who wouldn't try to bite some thug that was dragging them backward out of their favorite retreat?)

Sam Cooke, a forester, was marking timber up in the Asaph country one summer day. Foresters have a habit of never looking at the ground, even in rattlesnake country. They are always looking at tree trunks. As he made the trek from an oak trunk to a maple trunk, Sam felt some "funny ground" under his foot and, sensing what had happened, stretched his next stride. Glancing back, he saw the rattler scurrying away. He nearly did the same thing the following week. Sam let the critters live, even knowing that he would be marking timber throughout the area for several more weeks.

An entomologist, Gary Laudermilch, was looking at gypsy moth egg masses near Leetonia one August afternoon. He walked to within hugging distance of a white oak in order to see if the eggs had been parasitized. Gary glanced to the base of the tree and noticed a coiled yellow rattler. No buzz, no strike; the little fellow was just taking a snooze.

I met an elderly gentleman at the Bradley Wales Picnic Area one afternoon. He was with a small group gathered for a reunion. He pointed toward the nearby clearing and said, "I was raised in the house that stood there." I asked whether he remembered any encounters with rattlesnakes. He quickly responded, "My mother told me that she set me in the lawn one day when I was a toddler. A short while later, she came out to check on me and found me playing with a rattlesnake. She carried me into the house and returned to kill the snake."

Gary Dillman and I took some snakes to the Morris Rattlesnake Hunt one year, back when we were contemplating making an entry. We decided not to enter the snakes and were standing next to my truck, wondering what we were doing there. A middle-aged gentleman wearing a pastel tank top, white shorts, and a pair of flipflops walked over to us. He had thinning, fuzzy hair, wire-rimmed spectacles, and fingernails longer than any woman's I had ever seen. (When he approached, I am almost certain that Dillman drew the hammer back on his Smith.) The man asked if we would sell him a rattler, to which we agreed. Dropping the tailgate, I climbed into the back of the pickup and threw up the lid of our snake box. I asked him what he had in mind. He said, "Place your largest snake on the tailgate." ("Why not?" I thought. "I haven't seen a fool run like a stuck hog in a week or so.") I placed a plump forty-five-inch yellow phase on the tailgate. The Professor immediately placed his right hand around the snake's midsection, picked it up, and began talking to the serpent, while allowing it to rest its head and foresection on his left forearm. Never previously witnessing such a maneuver, I tensed up like a trout that had just been shocked by the fish biologist. I had visions of the snake suddenly recalling its recent tooth-chattering ride in the back of my short-bed Powerwagon. I also had visions of wailing sirens, a stupendous law suit, and a very tall state trooper handing me a citation with the charge of "reckless endangerment" written in very large capital letters. Realizing we were in the midst of a herd of screaming drunks, slamming car doors, and roaring Harleys, I was sure the Professor's term was running short; and there wasn't any time to open the debate on whether or not snakes hear.

The Professor calmly asked, "How much?"

Nearly speechless, I was able to utter, "Put it down and we'll talk," without moving my lips.

He laid the rattler on the tailgate. As I wiped the sweat from my brow, the Professor withdrew a business card from his wallet. The card identified him as a "poisonous" snake handler for a traveling sideshow. "People accuse me of using venomless snakes," he stated. "But as you can see, that's not true."

I should have paid the Professor the fifteen dollars. He had confirmed four axioms in a matter of seconds: timber rattlesnakes are generally nonaggressive; rattlers don't carry grudges; rattlers don't strike randomly at heat sources; one shouldn't judge a professor by his cover.

This snake handler obviously knew his business—I believe the long fingernails were tools of his trade. He could slip them under the snake and lift it without squeezing it. I shall never recommend that anyone attempt to free-handle a venomous snake; I will say that timber rattlesnakes are not nearly as dangerous as many people would lead us to believe. Those who masterfully grind the serpents with skidding tires could make a much cleaner kill by cracking the rattler's neck with a three-foot switch—a slender, green tree limb, for example. When one is using a firearm to stiffen a rattler, it's not necessary to fire from a distance of twenty or thirty feet, unless a potential ricochet is in question. The length of a shotgun is a safe distance from the largest of timber rattlers. If the snake decides to run for it and chooses your direction, you can easily sidestep it; it's not going to stop to bite you as it glides past. The fastest timber rattlers seldom attain a speed of three miles per hour when making their short-lived sprints.

I do fear rattlesnakes—to a point. I will never lose my respect for them. The possibility of being bitten by a timber rattler, when entering their territory, does exist, although minimally. You just need to use a little common sense.

• Wear leather high-tops when you're in rattlesnake country. I once observed a barefoot hiker on the Black Forest Trail in June, a peak month for timber rattlesnake activity. If the hiker had been bitten, I would have been forced to dispatch the culprit.

• To pitch camp at the base of a rockslide in timber rattler country during July, plus or minus three months, is witless.

• When you're in pit viper domain it's a good idea to look before you sit. Common sense should also steer you into doing a little investigating prior to reaching into a berry bush or sticking your hand into a rock crevice.

• If you have a camp or residence in timber rattlesnake country, keep your yard well groomed. If your property is a haven for mice, it's equally attractive to a rattler searching for a place to put on the fat.

• Exercise extreme caution when handling a "dead" rattler. A common prank involves luring a greenhorn into grasping a freshly beheaded rattler by the tail. The headless stump will quickly turn toward the clutching hand—far enough, at times, to make contact—resulting in a blood-curdling scream.

It takes a while for the "juice" to go out of these lanky harnesses of nerve and muscle. I witnessed the jaws of a detached head slash violently, fangs protruding, when poked with a stick a minute or so after the severance. Gary Dillman skinned and dressed a freshly killed rattler during a cookout. He washed the carcass in the nearby brook, put it in a plastic bag, and placed the bag on the ground. When the pot was ready, Gary reached for the bag, only to discover it was empty. He located the elongated chunk of meat, which was casually crawling through the woods, some twenty feet from camp.

Are timber rattlesnakes a problem in Northcentral Pennsylvania? I say no. Can people live, work, and play safely in the "rattler woods" if they use a little common sense? Yes. A sizable percentage of forest users enter our rattler woods unaware of the snake's preferred habitat, behavior, or even existence; there are few serious encounters. The possibility of such a person coming within striking range of a rattler is minimal. If it does happen, the snake will normally move in the opposite direction, "play possum," or become unnerved and rattle, allowing the intruder to back off. If surprised or pressured, the rattler may feign a strike. In event of a serious strike, a miss or glancing hit on a shoe or garment could be the result. Studies have indicated that when a rattler does make a successful connection, there is a 30 percent or greater chance that it will not inject venom; use of venom is a voluntary function related to feeding rather than to defense.

If you advocate the elimination of timber rattlers from the face of the earth, you won't lose many friends. If you are undecided, I hope to persuade you to examine all the evidence. If you are a timber rattlesnake lover like me, I advise you to speak softly when you're in a snake hunt town like Morris or Cross Fork; otherwise, you might find *your* name where *Crotalus horridus* used to be—on the government's list, "Species of Indeterminate Status."

4

In the Upper Ledges

O MANY, THE PHRASE "TIMBER RATTLESNAKE DEN" induces images best described with words like evil, hidden, dark, cold, damp, and pit. As a youngster, when someone mentioned a "rattler den," I imagined a cave surrounded by thorny ivy, rhododendron, and primeval conifers in the forest's enchanted sector; if you hunkered down, you could walk back in—providing you made it past the heap of hissing vipers guarding the entrance. Although I've never found a timber rattler in such a place, I still get the creeps when I explore a cave or old mine shaft. (Knowing it's in vain, I still check such places in hopes of discovering a rattlesnake gold mine, including the gold.)

On my inaugural snaking expedition, the nimble woodsman Ray Low introduced me to the requirements of a rattler denning area: the associated arrangement of topography, rock, and vegetation. When Ray located snakes, the required environmental denominators were always present. Later, when I commenced hunting on my own, I wasn't certain I had acquired an eye for rattler turf; then, when I crossed paths with seasoned rattlesnake captor John Howe, I knew Ray had taught me well.

Gary Wier, a noted rattlesnake hunter, is the author of a phrase that accurately describes ideal habitat for timber rattlesnakes. Gary was working the pit at the Morris Hunt one year, after entering his catch. As he displayed a large rattler, a woman's voice erupted from the droning crowd: "Where do you catch those things?"

"In the upper ledges," Gary neatly replied. It was a catchy one-liner to describe timber rattler denning areas.

Timber rattlesnakes, like other animals, require food and cover. These requirements are further specialized because of the snake's vulnerable design: it depends primarily on an outside heat source to accomplish simple life functions; it is slow moving and physically fragile; it poses little threat to a long list of predators. The bulk of a rattlesnake colony's population stays within a mile of home. "Home," the denning area, is a unique habitat upon which the perpetuation of this species depends and which is confined to a relatively minute acreage of the species' general range.

Typically in the mountainous portions of Northcentral Pennsylvania, blocks and boulders of rock accumulate on slopes and at the bases of rock exposures—ledges and outcrops. Fissures and pockets in these exposures and the rock rubble create ideal settings for rattlesnake dens.

Some parts of this region of the Appalachian Plateaus have been glaciated. Several times within the last two million years, thick ice sheets have moved into Pennsylvania from the north, extensively scouring and sculpting the land's surface as they advanced and depositing voluminous amounts of debris as they retreated. Over millions of years, the combined effects of glaciers, running water, and the downward movement of debris under the influence of gravity have resulted in the smoothly rounded uplands and deep, angular valleys we see today. Numerous contoured outcroppings of sedimentary rocks, including red shales and green and gray, fine-grained sandstones (sometimes quarried for flagstone) are evident on the rugged slopes. In addition, exposures of thicker beds of conglomeratic sandstone and of gray to white, coarse-grained sandstone tend to produce large blocks as debris upon weathering. Most rattlesnake hunters refer to these thin-layered, fine-grained deposits as *shalerock* and the coarser material as *boulder rock*.

We further classify shalerock and boulder rock according to

its form: a *slide* is a heavy deposit of fragmented rock; *rubble* is scattered fragments or minislides; an *outcropping* is a chunk of rock protruding from the ground—if it's steep-faced and on a sidehill, it's a *ledge*. Further classification refers to size and uses high-tech terminology: *small, good-sized,* and *huge.*

The available combinations of den rock terminology would be mind-boggling to a timber rattlesnake, if it could hear. The

snakes don't seem to prefer a particular composition of rock for use as denning or basking areas. If the location, size, and arrangement of rock provides cover from predators, a means of efficiently regulating body temperature (adjacent hot and cool areas), and a place to hibernate (beneath the frost line), the site could be utilized as a den—providing it is next to a suitable foraging area. In Northcentral Pennsylvania, rock forms utilized as dens are surrounded by hardwood forests (the "timber" in the rattlesnake's name) which support the snake's favorite morsels, including voles, mice, chipmunks, and small birds. Thus, the serpents need not search far.

Of equal importance to a den's location relative to a food source is its location relative to direct sunlight. All the rock in the world would be of little value to a timber rattler if it were starving for solar rays. Lots of sun, when called for, must be available to rattlers, especially the gravid females. They spend most of the summer gestating at basking areas, regulating their body temperatures to promote optimum development of the eggs they carry. The basking site is also the birthing site. If the entrance to the winter den cavity *(hibernaculum)* is shaded, a sunny summer den (basking area) must be close by in order for the site to be productive. Birthing is in late summer; the newborns must be able to reach the hibernaculum.

The aspect (the direction a slope faces) is one sunlight factor determining the productivity of a timber rattler *deme* (individual colony). Although southern exposures are most productive, rattler dens can be found on a variety of aspects, provided other solar conditions are favorable. Slope position, the second sunlight factor, is also critical due to the rugged topography of the Northcentral region. The steep-sided mountains are abundantly trimmed with hog-back ridges, hollows, and ravines. Relief often varies thirteen hundred feet in a horizontal mile, with localized features exhibiting 50 to 60 percent slopes. Otherwise "good snake rock" is useless to the rattlers when it is positioned low on the slope where the beams of light arrive late and depart early.

A third light factor is the density of tall shrubs and trees growing on a potential denning area. If the canopy is closed (shoulder to shoulder), the rocks will be shaded during most of the basking season—throughout the season if the trees are evergreens. Since the hibernaculum, basking area, and birthing location must be in close proximity for this species to endure, an area of rockslides or ledges overtopped by dense timber fails to qualify.

The upper portions of the Mountainous High Plateau's sunny slopes provide the better locations for timber rattlesnake denning areas. The soil has a relatively low moisture content; the trees are often stunted and sparse. Understory vegetation (blueberry, fern, laurel), responsive to the sunny conditions, covers the forest floor, preventing regeneration of the taller species. This low brush provides cover for the rattlers while allowing the needed sunlight to penetrate into numerous pockets. Defoliating forest pests such as oak leaf rollers, gypsy moths, and the assembly of elusive factors causing maple dieback seem to thrive on the sunny upper slopes; they knock a few more holes in the already thin overstory. Periodic ice storms wreak further havoc on these elevated woodlands.

In addition, most Northcentral Pennsylvania slopes have experienced a wildfire or two within the last century. Fuel, weather, and topography (factors that influence the behavior of wildfires) are most favorable to fires on the upper slopes. Often, the fires burned "hot and deep," further reducing the sites' tree-growing capacities. Therefore, the chances of finding an exposed rock formation—and rattlers—are greater in the upper ledges.

In Northcentral Pennsylvania, the timber rattlesnake spends most of its life—roughly October through April each year—in its hibernaculum, a frost-free cavity. It is difficult to say how far beneath the surface a rattlesnake den must be, other than "below the frost line." The line at any given site varies from year to year, depending on the severity of the winter. A severely snowy winter could result in only minor frost penetration—the blanket of snow serves as insulation—but during a severely cold winter with little snow, the frost line would be deeper. Another factor to consider is the composition and design of the hibernaculum. In a pure talus slide there are numerous crevices for the cold air to penetrate because it lacks insulating soil or leaf litter. There, the frost line would be deeper than in a neighboring area of talus or small outcroppings mixed with soil and covered with humus and litter. The aspect of the site also influences frost penetration. Timber rattlesnake dens are found on exposures normally ranging from southeast to west, and frost penetration would thus vary.

Using radiotelemetry, Howard Reinert (1992, personal communication) discovered that twenty-eight of thirty hibernacula in his Southeastern Pennsylvania study were in wooded sites— the chamber entrance was beneath a forest canopy, and the surface rock was mixed with soil and partially covered by humus and leaf litter. Open basking sites were readily available, however. The remainig two hibernacula were located in open rocks with no overhead canopy, but they were at the fringe, where humus and leaf litter were encroaching.

Reinert believes that the presence of moisture in the hibernaculum may be critical to hibernating timber rattlers. He noted that, upon emergence, the snakes were coated with a thin layer of mud—their chambers were damp, at least.

Several times I have observed twelve to sixteen adult snakes grouped on a talus slope or at a ledge crevice early in the emergence period—I suspect that the individuals of each group shared the same hibernaculum. William H. Martin, a timber rattlesnake ecologist, refers to these main hibernacula as "communal ancestral dens" to which the individual rattlesnakes show high fidelity (Martin 1992, 263, 259).

Some denning areas contain numerous hibernacula scattered throughout an acre or more of suitable ground—the reason I use "denning area" rather than "den" to describe a rattlesnake colony's home base. On May 2, 1993, my party observed eighteen adult snakes that had just emerged from hibernation. They were in groups of one to three individuals, well spaced throughout a two-hundred-yard-long, rocky, partly wooded portion of a south-facing mountain rim. The snakes that we disturbed retreated far into their crevices.

Generally summarizing the timber rattlesnake's denning area requirements in Northcentral Pennsylvania: (1) a hibernating chamber where a proper range of temperature and, perhaps, moisture content prevails during the hibernation season (October through April); (2) a rocky, sunny basking area at or near the hibernaculum entrance, where the snakes can bring their bodily functions to order upon emerging (April 30—shading by hardwoods is not a factor until after the mid-May green-up); (3) a rocky, sunny basking site within several hundred yards of the hibernaculum, where gravid females can gestate and give birth (June-September 20). This site will also be used by other members of the population to facilitate molting (protection and thermoregulation when preparing to shed skin) and by snakes that are dispersing toward and returning from the summer foraging range (Brown 1993).

Traversing the summer slopes, one may discover denning and basking sites at various locations. When Gary Dillman and I first hunted on Hershey Kiss Mountain, we started at an elevation of eight hundred feet, the base of the triangular point. Ascending the point we inspected a patch of small shalerock rubble that was shaded by white oak and red pine; there was no evidence of rattlers. At thirteen hundred feet we entered a quarter-acre open slide of larger shalerock where we observed six rattlers. Above the slide, we climbed through a shalerock ledge partially shaded by red and white pines—again, no sign of snakes. Farther up the slope we checked an area where boulder-rock rubble, huckleberries, and scattered chestnut oak prevailed; we found three juveniles. At sixteen hundred feet the point benched. Scouting the next pitch, we discovered a medium-sized boulder-rock slide. It looked superior, snake-wise, but we failed to locate rattlers. At nineteen hundred feet we combed a plot of small shalerock ledges and mountain laurel. Oak "wolf" trees—large, open-grown trees with sprawling limbs—were soaking up most of the available sunlight. Our search there was fruitless.

I returned to Kiss Mountain about ten years later. The lower shalerock slide had been raked over by snake hunters; I saw one snake. I couldn't find any in the boulder-rock rubble where Gary and I had spotted the juvenile snakes. There were twelve rattlers in the upper boulder-rock slide (we may have overlooked the den rock on our first visit). In the high plot of small shalerock ledges, the wolf trees had succumbed to forest pests. A plump adult timber rattler was basking at one of the newly sunlit ledges.

Savanna Ridge is a northeast to southwest appendage to a broad north-south ridge. At the head of the hollow forming Savanna's southeastern flank, Gary and I found several rattlers in a small sphere of boulder rubble. Hunting the southeastern flank of the ridge, we discovered scattered "borderline" out-croppings, nearly overtopped by an oak canopy. On the ridge's point, a small snake lay in an opening of boulder rubble. Drop-ping down the point, we came into dense shade, as the red oaks were thriving. We swung around the point to its northwestern flank and climbed back to the rim. The habitat appeared good as we entered a region of savannalike openings carpeted with huckleberry, sweet fern, scattered pitch pine, and small boulder-rock outcroppings. We observed seven rattlers throughout this aromatic oasis speckled with blooming mountain pink. Suc-cessive hunts on Savanna have produced up to twenty sightings (good by today's standards for our locale).

Some timber rattlers, headed for favorite foraging grounds, leave the denning areas shortly after emerging from hiberna-tion. The snakes, dispersing in all directions—upslope, down-slope, or across the slope—will utilize a variety of habitats throughout or adjacent to the timbered ridges. (Those traveling to the valley floors are periodically noticed by people who decide they have come down for water. Funny, since the snakes' relatives may be spending the summer on an arid mountaintop a mile from the nearest water hole.)

Timber rattlesnake hunters have occasional luck finding the snakes around old stone fencerows, foundations, and rock formations on abandoned, or edge, farmland. Such productive areas are normally on the lower slopes of traditional snake ridges. Often, large rattlers that inhabit these rodent hotels for the summer are incidentally encountered by farmers and other local residents. Stories of rattlers being beheaded by the hay mower, to be packaged several days later by the baler, are quite common in the farming villages of the Big Woods. (A rattler traveling through high grass, or investigating a commotion, would elevate its head several or more inches.) Other hunters concentrate their efforts in clear-cuts, as well as natural expanses of low brush, finding that the snakes utilize old stumps, logs, and occasional boulders as summer headquarters.

The locations of established rattlesnake crossings along certain roads were common knowledge at one time, although sightings at the crossings have decreased drastically in recent years. On summer evenings, as the air temperature drops, a passing rattler will stretch out on a roadway to soak up a few more hours of heat. (The forest floor, being shaded all day, is cooler.) Sometimes, a snake will establish temporary residency along a forest road, using the road as a basking site.

Other human constructions also attract timber rattlers. Flagstone quarrying in the past has created rocky openings throughout the Northcentral mountains. Waste rock was pushed off these sidehill quarry flats, creating slides of tailings. Rattlers use some of the slides as basking areas; where the tailings are deep, the snakes appear to have established permanent dens. The piles of fallen timber at abandoned coal mines and sawmills provide attractive summer dwellings for rattlers; likewise do appliance dumps in the older, unreclaimed strip-mine pits—

all eyesores that are fading as our environmental awareness evolves. The snuggery of a junked car, placed in the rattler's domain, is savored by rattlers as summer headquarters—some hunting clubs place "junkers" throughout their property for use as blinds during deer season. I refer to one denning area as the Junked Car Den. After looking through the outcroppings, I check the trunk, engine, and passenger compartments of the nearby Plymouth. It's always littered with skins and usually holds a rattler in one of the three wards. Rattlers will also choose a backyard lumber pile or outbuilding as a seasonal abode.

Although the timber rattlesnake adapts to a variety of summer habitats, the absence of the specialized denning area suitable for hibernation, basking, and birthing will render a region void of rattlers. Throughout the snake's general range, including portions of the Northcentral Big Woods, large tracts of the hilly, forested plateau are rattler-free. One such area is Armenia Mountain, the headwaters of the Tioga River. Ledges on the mountain's sunny aspects are scarce. Soil and local climatic influences support dense stands of northern hardwoods. (The virgin timber included a high percentage of closely fit, towering white pines and hemlocks.) Open areas are primarily wetlands, trimmed with highbush blueberry, alder, hardhack, and occasional firs. A few of the open rock outcroppings radiate a borderline "feeling of rattlesnake." I suspect that, if they ever harbored small rattler colonies, early settlers may have exterminated them; however, I never heard or read about rattlesnake encounters during Armenia's settlement era.

Experienced timber rattlesnake hunters concentrate on locating productive configurations of rock, sunlight, and vegetation when searching through potential denning areas. They often sense the presence of snakes well before they see or hear one. A trained eye will spot a partially exposed rattler basking in a maze of rocks and brush at a distance of fifty yards; the hunter zeroes in first on the suspect rock, then looks for the snake. When guiding individuals desiring to observe their first rattler in the wild, even in new territory, the hunter will instruct, "Check that rock over there," allowing each newcomer to find the first snake.

Healthy oak,
I'm on the foot of the slope,
Rattler fledge,
I'll be on the upper ledge.

5

Lifestyle of C. horridus

EVEN THE DULLEST OF CREATURES INHABITING THE Black Forest has inherited the ability to produce spine-tingling sounds at the most opportune moments. The woodnotes that drive me berserk are ones erupting from an unknown source, made by what I've guessed to be either a bear or a tree frog, or possibly something in between—perhaps a hobgoblin.

While hunting rattlers one day, I happened upon a couple of fuzzy, white, vulture chicks. Their nest was an old porcupine den under a shalerock ledge. I couldn't believe the sound they made when I invaded their space. I related the story to Tim Clifton, who was planning an environmental discovery field trip for his Youth Conservation Corps crew. We made plans to take the students to the nest without telling them what they were to observe, hoping that the birds would repeat the sounds I'd heard. The following day, we approached the ledge from the downhill side. The entrance to the crevice was hidden by lush weedy growth, thanks to the porcupines. I rattled a stick on the ledge, and the birds quickly replied. The kids' guesses concerning the animal occupying the cavity included bear, panther, and wolf. They all finally agreed that it was a bobcat. They were amazed when they saw the downy bambinos that were making the "bobcat growls."

A wide range of animals, man included, is capable of emitting a few universally understood vocables like the buzzards' "keep your distance" growl. I heard a peculiar growl one day when

Dick Hamblin and I were hunting rattlers near Middlebury Center. We were working our way through a steep section of small shalerock ledges and huckleberries. When I stopped for a breather, I heard a sound that I only instinctively recognized; although I couldn't visualize its source, my neck hackles stood on end. It sounded like a combination of a stiff breeze swirling through a pine thicket, a balloon being inflated, and Hamblin's stomach when he's five minutes overdue for lunch. Although hard to describe, the message was clear. Realizing there were no pines or balloons in close proximity and Dick was sixty yards to my right, I was temporarily stymied. I heard the warning again, still unable to determine the source. I scanned a semicircle at a range of ten to thirty feet, then focused in on closer ground. At the base of a small outcropping, sprawled across a low shrub, and about two feet from my kneecap, lay a big, "flat" rattler. Upon exhaling, the snake rounded out; then it didn't look so big and ferocious—on the contrary, it was a rather smallish specimen. It never rattled or struck. When I reached for it with my stick, it headed for its hole. I had been hissed upon.

The next time I heard the now familiar rattlesnake hiss I was frightened, to say the least. I was standing in waist-high laurel near a boulder-rock outcropping. Remembering how close I'd been to the other puffing viper, I quickly scoured the striking-range pad I was standing on—nothing. I was baffled until the noisy fellow growled again and I spotted him lying on a slab about twenty feet distant. It was a large rattler, apparently capable of projecting its hiss over such a distance.

Timber rattlesnakes employ numerous defense tactics besides the hissing trick. The most common tactic is the "swish." "Swish" describes the sound produced by a rattler's tail as it hastily disappears into a secure rock bunker. Often, on hot, sunny days, the snakes lie only partially exposed at the entrance of their favorite shelter rock. (When air and surface temperatures are approaching eighty degrees Fahrenheit, too much direct sunlight would kill the snakes.) The snakes, at optimum operating temperature, scurry for cover quickly when approached. Hunting rattlers in the denning areas on those hot, sunny days usually results in "swish counting."

The buzz of a rattler whirling its appendage of segmented, heavily cornified epidermis is a startling sound that can induce a brief spasm within even a seasoned snake hunter. It is an impressive warning to an intruder, man or beast. Rattlers don't rattle to hypnotize chipmunks. They rattle when they are scared. Other species of snakes also exhibit a quivering tail when unnerved. Perhaps it lures the predator to grab for the "wrong" end of the snake? There are numerous theories.

When sensing potential danger in the open, timber rattlers often lie motionless, relying on their natural camouflage to conceal them. If the snake "cracks," it may make a run for it or slip into a tight defensive coil. If further harassed, the snake may feign a strike. Normally, a rattler will bite an adversary only as a last resort.

It is interesting to approach a group of basking rattlers that are scattered about, several feet from their den rock. One snake will start buzzing and make a move, then the others simultaneously join in. If you stand between them and their rock, they'll go around you or across your feet, intent on reaching the safety of their crevice. The closer they get to safety, the faster they go; slowing down to give you a fang or two is the last thing on their minds. If pressured, when on the run, an excited timber rattler will do just about anything to elude its pursuer. I've used my stick time and again to catch semi-airborne snakes that were en route to certain death. Once, a novice hunter attempted to capture a black rattler on a high ledge. The snake scooted six feet across the flat ledge top and into the atmosphere, landing on the crown of a thirty-foot birch tree growing from the base of the ledge.

It is hard to predict when or why a timber rattler will choose to lie still, rattle, coil, run, or strike. The defensive tactic employed is seemingly governed by the availability and type of cover, the snake's metabolic state, the intruder's method of approach, and, perhaps, the snake's individual traits.

Like other animals, timber rattlesnakes occasionally display curiosity. The yellow rattler of Carjack Point is one example. Each year, Gary Dillman and I would visit Carjack to inventory the rattlers. On our first five inspections we always checked a scenic little shalerock ledge midway up the point. The ledge is in an opening, faces the sun, has lots of fissures, and is framed by lowbush blueberries—an ideal setting. We couldn't understand why snakes weren't using the site. On our sixth trek past the ledge, a four-inch-square hole, positioned at eye level on the sheer face of the rock, caught my attention. Using a reflector, I directed a midmorning beam of sunshine into the hole. In the corner of the "room" within, I shined the flank of a yellow rattler. Keeping the light trained on the snake, I called for Gary. Soon the placid rattler eased forth, crawling toward my solar flashlight and stopping only when its nose was flush with the entrance. When I removed the light, the snake retreated to its chambers. When I shined the cavity again, the snake returned, its tongue flicking busily (smelling).

Gary and I decided to check out a favorite denning area on Big Ridge one morning. I crept onto a vantage point above the basking area in order to observe the rattlers as Gary approached from below their rock. There were nine rattlers scattered about in various poses. When Gary climbed the steep slope toward the snakes, forty some feet away, several rattlers raised their heads about six inches. As he zigzagged across the rocks, the snakes turned their heads in concert, following his every move. They tucked low and sat tight as Gary neared the contour where he could see them.

While some rattlers seem indifferent to the approach of a human, others, at the slightest hint of danger, vanish silently into their hideaway, leaving not a trace. Although the snakes are instinctively afraid of large intruders, a narrow escape from a hawk, fox, snake hunter, or other predator is most likely responsible for creating an extra-wary individual. One such skittish (or smart) rattler used the top of a shalerock ledge on Laurel Ridge for its summer headquarters. The ledge top slopes gently with the steeper sidehill; it holds a precariously clinging red pine, which gives it a plush topping of fallen needles. In the middle of this four-by-four pad, about a foot from the pine's trunk, a slight step in the ledge top forms a narrow horizontal crevice; the opening faces up the slope. For years I suspected that a timber rattler was using the crevice, even though on repeated visits I found nothing. One day I checked the ledge and, as usual, continued working my way up the point. I was on the ridge top for about twenty minutes, then began retracing my steps down to the red pine ledge, contrary to my normal hunting route. When I was within twenty-five yards of the ledge, I began stalking. When the laurel thinned enough to allow me to see the ledge top, I stopped to study the crevice area; I was about fifty feet out. The bed of needles was mottled by sunlight filtering through the pine's scraggly boughs. The area appeared vacant, as usual. I took several steps, my eyes still intently trained on the spot. As I moved, so did a yellow phase rattler that had lain facing me, about two feet upslope from the crevice. Taking advantage of the incline, with a few graceful whips, the snake slipped tail-first into the fissure. I raced over and peered into the crack, seeing only the cap of a chestnut oak acorn. I banged my stick on the entrance of the cavity. The only reply was the sea shell whisper of the distant tumbling run.

I've heard tales of rattlesnake dens having such a putrid stench that visitors become a bit queasy, at least, and sometimes violently ill. I've personally observed several snake hunters become a bit sick at denning areas—one was nauseous after he slipped, striking his elbow on a boulder; another was dizzy after pushing his cardiovascular system to the limit; the third hunter was faint, suffering from a hangover. For a human, I have a keen sense of smell, yet I couldn't smell anything out of the ordinary at those sites—or at any other rattlesnake den. If you're ever at a rattlesnake roundup and think you're getting an occasional whiff of serpent odor, it's probably just a human being standing upwind. However, if you handle a snake bare-handed you will notice a somewhat rancid odor on your hands, even after you wash them several times (it's psychological after the second washing). This pungent odor is often emitted from scent glands in the tail when the snake is being captured or handled.

Timber rattlesnake hunters are often asked, "How far can they strike?" The reply I usually give is, "They can strike accurately at one-third their length, possibly hit you at one-half their length, and probably miss you at the snake's length." But like any such formula, this one is only an approximation. The experienced snake hunter approaches each rattler as an individual potential hazard. (As I said before, timber rattlers are normally docile, but only fools lose their respect for them.) Things to consider when calculating the striking range of an individual rattler at a given moment include the snake's size, pose, mood, metabolic rate, and position relative to the possible target. With a little experience, one can quickly size up a situation, determining the closest safe distance according to changing conditions.

Timber rattlesnakes are not known to accomplish miraculous feats. A four-footer can be easily handled with a three-foot snake stick. I don't recommend that anybody should "play" with venomous snakes, but momentarily placing one's hand several inches in front of a fully stretched rattler wouldn't be much of a risk. If one understands the snake's limitations—and acknowledges one's own—there is virtually no danger in approaching or handling a timber rattler. In almost every case (perhaps in all cases), when a timber rattlesnake "hunter" is bitten, the headline should read "Daredevil Is Bitten." Those avoidable incidents seldom occur in rattlesnake habitat. They happen in front of spectators in a backyard or on a fairground when the handler, trying to impress an audience, takes a chance—and loses. The snake, dislocated from its ancestral niche and operating on instinct, always gets the blame.

Another question commonly asked by those unfamiliar with rattlers is, "Must they be coiled to strike?" I usually reply that a rattlesnake can *bite* from any position, providing it can maneuver its mouth onto the target. For example, an outstretched rattler that is firmly grasped at its midsection by a hand or snake pincer will quickly make a U-turn and bite the trammel. A *strike*, in contrast, is considered to be the action of a rattler taking careful aim and thrusting its head, mouth agape, at its target. But in order to lash forth, the snake must be in a stance with its head pulled back, its anterior in an S-shape. A snake that perceives a serious threat may further refine this stance by slipping into a *striking coil* configuration. It draws its posterior half into a nearly complete circle, its tail facing the adversary. Over this base, the snake spirals its anterior half into an S-shape; its head squarely faces the target. The pose is designed so that none of the snake's loops will crimp shut as it strikes. The snake is swollen, primed for action, and able to attain its maximum controlled striking distance.

In contrast, a rattler can strike only a short distance from a *resting coil*—a posture often taken by a rattler when sleeping or basking. This coil is flat and relaxed. The posterior base circle is absent; the tail is often near the center of the coil. Some of the snake's anterior is lying on the ground, forming part of the coil's outer circle. The coil's midsection loop is closed—it cannot be extended to contribute power and distance during a strike, but would kink and act as a drag. "Experiments with a piece of hose coiled to simulate a rattler in its resting coil will show that a forward lunge for any distance will twist the head laterally, thus illustrating the unsuitability of this type of coil for a strike" (Klauber 1972, 478).

If a timber rattlesnake is provoked while in a resting coil, it may quickly modify its posture to a *defensive coil*, short of a well-formed striking coil. The snake establishes a circular base with its posterior, while positioning more of its anterior on top in a flat S-shape (as opposed to the spiral of a striking coil); this is

RATTLESNAKE COILS

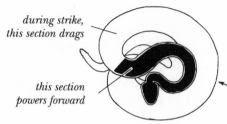

during strike, this section drags

this section powers forward

RESTING
(relaxed, slouched; midsection loop kinks during strike)

midlength

midlength

DEFENSIVE
(Stacked, leveled; more anterior contributes to strike, but midsection loop still kinks)

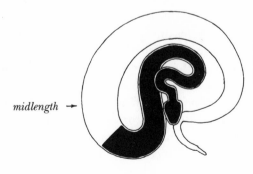

midlength

STRIKING
(Spirals up; all loops open)

better suited for striking than the resting coil, but a closed loop near the midsection still restricts the striking distance.

A related question is, "Do they always rattle before they strike?" Left unmolested in the wild, the only striking a rattler does is for the purpose of obtaining food. If the snake buzzed every time it intended to strike its prey, it would probably die of starvation in a year or so. Nor do I believe a rattler would intentionally warn a hawk that was lifting it from its basking rock. I suppose this question is intended to mean "Do they always rattle before they strike a person?" No. If a timber rattler is surprised by a crushing foot or reaching hand, the strike before the rattle should be expected—it is the snake's instinctive reaction to an attack. But if it is aware of the approaching attacker it will almost always rattle and otherwise threaten before it will strike.

Timber rattlers are proficient swimmers, as I learned in my first encounter—the rattler that I saw in Blockhouse Creek. Another swimmer episode was witnessed by Gary Dillman during the summer of 1982. Gary was boating about the Tioga Lake, taking water samples. Entering the lake's Mill Creek Arm, he noticed a snake that was a hundred yards offshore and beelining for the far side. Typical of snake/boat encounters, when Gary moved in for a closer look, the snake tried to climb aboard; it was a fifty-inch-class yellow rattler. Gary said the snake was "at home in the water"—the newly constructed reservoir had proved no barrier to this oldtimer's established summer prowling pattern. Perhaps the desire for mates and food (probably in that order) fuels the snakes through uncomfortable encounters with cool water. When comfort is the order of the day, cool water is not well received: on a sunny June 2, I headed for a den site overlooking the lower Pine Creek Gorge. When I was within a quarter mile of the den, a thunderstorm rapidly approached. As I arrived at a ledge above the basking area, lightning was already hammering the ridge. I noticed a dozen rattlers scattered through the basking area, a rockless opening of grasses and huckleberries about ten feet downslope from the ledge. Risking all, I stood on the ledge in order to watch the snakes' reactions when the rain struck. (My other option was to stand beneath a towering white pine.) The snakes weren't bothered by the flashing and crackling, but when the shower commenced, they made a frantic run for the ledge. Within minutes, the storm passed; the snakes promptly emerged from the shelter.

Although timber rattlesnakes are labeled as yellow (light) phase or black (dark) phase, there is a variety of color shades within these two extremes. Some individuals appear to be borderline (intermediate), in color. The best indicator of a rattler's color phase is the color of its eye—a yellow-gold iris in the yellow phase, dark gray in the other. In both, the tail (vent to rattle) is black. Newborn timbers are all colored and patterned in a similar fashion, basically gray with darker crossbands that are described as chevrons, saddles, or blotches. When the infant sheds its skin, its genetically determined color phase becomes evident.

The underside of a yellow rattler is generally cream colored. Its backside may be patternless, ranging from pure sulphur to brown or olive, but more typically it will have chocolate brown crossbands on a light brown to yellow background. A black rattler's belly is basically white, with a dusting of gray and a sprinkling of pepper. A "velvet-black" rattler, common to our Northcentral mountains, has a patternless black backside—a recent shedding producing the plush, velvety appearance. But the typical black phase rattler carries black crossbands on a gray background. In some, the bands are trimmed with lemon yellow against a background of raw umber, giving them the appearance of a yellow rattler at first glance.

Color is not an indicator of the snake's sex. Some studies have suggested that the type of cover available in a given locale, or its microclimate, may account for the predominance of light or dark rattlers in that area. The literature suggests that in the cooler, heavily forested uplands of the timber rattler's range the percentage of black phase rattlers is at its greatest. Of the 206 rattlers I observed in Northcentral Pennsylvania between April 1988 and July 1991, 30 percent were yellow phases. However, my do-it-yourself study was quite uncontrolled; the observations were primarily on sunny basking sites and I probably overlooked a higher percentage of yellow snakes—they blend well with the sunny forest floor. In addition, a percentage of snakes is often hidden while the others are exposed.

Timber rattlesnakes have an unmerited reputation for being blind and striking indiscriminately when they are getting ready to shed. A week or so prior to casting its outer epidermis, a snake's vision is clouded while its new protective eye shield is forming (the old one will be shed with the outer skin). In addition, an oily secretion between the old and new skins assists in the molting process, further impairing the snake's vision. True to their nature, snakes in this condition prefer to be left alone, normally striking only when antagonized. "Milky-eyed" rattlers exhibit an action I call "reverse striking"; they jerk their heads back to avoid a waving snake stick or foot. If given the opportunity, they will move away slowly (due to the impaired vision). When pressured into hasty retreat, these snakes often make wild, spastic movements as they near obstacles along the escape route. An inexperienced observer may interpret the sudden agitations as being strikes.

Unlike humans, who shed flakes of old skin constantly, the timber rattler periodically casts its entire outer skin, normally at least once a year. A more active rattler may shed several times. Shedding frequency is thought to be more directly related to a snake's feeding rate and metabolism, rather than to its growth rate. When shedding begins, the skin is loosened first at the snake's head. As the snake crawls forth, the old skin turns inside out. In many instances, it appears as though the snake snags the head skin on rocks or brush; it is not essential to the operation.

The hardened, thickened skin (keratin) covering the living terminus of the rattler's tail (the matrix) is also cast, but remains loosely interlocked to the matrix—a new rattle segment has been added. The first time an infant rattler sheds, the minuscule first rattle segment produced is called the button. As the rattler grows, so does the matrix; thus, each new segment, upon shedding, is slightly larger than the previous one. Thus, a growing rattler will have a tapered rattle. An older snake, with minimal

SHEDDING

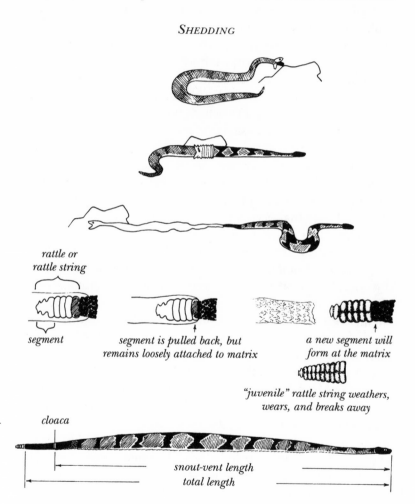

rattle or
rattle string

segment

segment is pulled back, but
remains loosely attached to matrix

a new segment will
form at the matrix

"juvenile" rattle string weathers,
wears, and breaks away

cloaca

snout-vent length
total length

growth rate, carries a uniform rattle in which each segment is the same size; the tapered section produced in its youth is lost to weather, wear, and breakage. It is uncommon for a wild timber rattler to carry a rattle having more than a dozen segments, although it may produce threefold that in its lifetime.

Various other species of snakes share basking locations with timber rattlers. I've observed red-bellied and garter snakes in close proximity to rattlers. Some of my favorite hunting areas are at the perimeter of copperhead range. At one site, I saw a green snake, several rattlers, and a copperhead in a group. Dangling within a foot of one rattler, the green snake was suspended in a laurel bush. As I approached, the rattlers and the copperhead scooted under the same rock.

Unable to perform the acrobatics of some snake species, timber rattlers are, nevertheless, good climbers. Several times I have seen them strung through branches of mountain laurel, basking three feet off the ground. I once noticed one perched on an oak tree that had tipped to form a twenty degree incline. The snake was coiled next to a stub about twenty feet up the trunk and seven feet above the forest floor—it wasn't much of a climbing feat, but it looked a bit uncommon. I've never observed one in a shrub or tree where a vertical climb on a limbless trunk was required; however, I recently heard that such is possible (Reinert 1992, personal communication). I removed the prettiest velvet-black rattler I've ever seen from a small storage shed behind Clyde Rouse's place near Ansonia. I still can't figure out how it reached the shelf on top of the smooth wall.

The truth about the length of timber rattlesnakes is often stretched, even after the snake itself is literally stretched. Although stories of six-foot rattlers are common in Northcentral Pennsylvania, I have yet to observe a timber rattlesnake, dead or alive, head and rattles included, that reaches five feet in length. Upon investigation, stories about the death or capture of an alleged behemoth usually end with "Oh, I can't remember who told me," or "Oh, that was last year and we threw it in the crick," or "Oh, we really didn't measure it, we estimated the length of each of the four pieces."

Perhaps the six-foot rattler story is generated as follows: First, take a fifty-four-inch live rattler (that is one inch shorter than the largest timber rattler ever entered at the Morris Rattlesnake Hunt). Kill it and leave it on the hot pavement until all the life is out of it and it's nice and soft. Now, stretch it for all it's worth and measure it—fifty-seven inches. Don't forget the rattles, they're two more. Since it's so close, round it up to sixty inches. Now, tell a few people about it. As the story becomes second and third hand, the conversion from sixty inches to six feet is automatic. If you've worked the skin up well, it will match the story, especially if you say it shrank a bit before you tacked it to the board. (Several days after writing this chapter, I was talking snake with a retired Pine Creek forest ranger. He said, "The largest rattler I ever killed was fifty-six inches." Then he added, "Yessir, just four inches shy of six feet.")

In Northcentral Pennsylvania, rattlers generally emerge from their den cavities during the latter part of April, providing there is warmth (temperatures in the sixties) and sunshine on the surface. Within two weeks following the general emergence date, a few reports of large rattlers being spotted, captured, or killed along the valley floors are not uncommon. It seems as though some of the snakes emerge from their dens and promptly glide down the slopes with reckless abandon. These sightings occur when the nights are still chilly. Perhaps these large, early roamers are heading for productive feeding grounds and, due to their bulk and superior mobility (as opposed to smaller specimens), are less threatened by the sometimes fluctuating spring weather. Within another week or two, the early reports subside.

The majority of snakes, upon emergence, spend several or more weeks in the security of the basking areas. The sunbathing brings the rattler's bodily functions to order, helping to stifle parasites; the rocks, warmed by day, buffer the cool spring nights. During mid to late June, a flurry of molting activity occurs, followed by an evident dispersal. Gravid females, who will give birth during late summer, congregate at choice basking rocks (sometimes called summer dens, gestating rocks, birthing rocks, or mother rocks). Small rattlers scatter about through the basking areas or move a short distance into the surrounding timber; older snakes might range to over a mile. Rattler sightings throughout the forest and adjoining lands increase from late June through August as the adults forage about and seek mates.

Several anatomical features aid the rattlesnake in procuring its prey. One is a pair of heat sensors, the pit organs, which are unique to the pit vipers—copperheads and rattlesnakes in Pennsylvania. A pit is a cavity $\frac{1}{8}$ inch in diameter and $\frac{3}{16}$ inch deep with a forward-facing external opening. There is one on each side of the snake's head, between the nostril and the eye. At the rear of the cavity there is a concave membrane, like a satellite TV dish. A nerve linking the dish to the snake's brain responds to minute, sudden changes in infrared radiation. This allows the rattler to pinpoint warm-blooded prey up to a distance of eighteen inches in total darkness. Recent study suggests that pit vipers actually see images generated by the pit organs.

Another feature, the Jacobson's organ, is located on the roof of the snake's mouth. It is a receptor for scents carried in by the flicking tongue. This, combined with a conventional sense of smell, gives the snake exceptional tracking ability.

The timber rattlesnake's fangs are $\frac{1}{2}$ inch long, at most, in large specimens. These hollow, elongated teeth, through which venom is delivered, are folded back, up to the roof of the mouth, except during a strike; they also hinge down independently to assist, like claws, when the snake swallows prey. Replacement fangs are always in store; the rattler might shed several pair during the active season.

The venom is manufactured in two glands, one located just below and mostly posterior to each eye. During a strike, the snake voluntarily controls the injection of venom—through both, either, or neither fang. The venom immobilizes, kills, and starts digesting the prey. Rattler venom is called hemorrhagic, hemolytic, or hemotoxic—it destroys blood and muscle tissue and carries shock-enducing agents.

In their preferred feeding grounds, timber rattlesnakes use their highly developed sense of smell to locate runways frequented by mice and voles. White-footed mice, in particular, run along the tops of fallen logs, especially under the cover of darkness. A hunting rattler, after choosing a "hot" log, will coil next to it, resting its head on the log (Reinert Posture, see chapter 6). The snake will lie—perhaps sleep—in this ambush position for hours. Awakened by the vibrations on the log, and guided by vision and the pit organs, the alerted rattler homes in on the passing mouse. In a blurred and often delicate action, it strikes the mouse, injects venom, releases, and returns to its prestrike posture. The bite may actually be a "stab"—the lower jaw doesn't have to clamp; the whole design spares the snake a retaliatory attack. The stricken mouse may take a hop, sometimes several, before becoming immobile; and, usually within a minute, it succumbs. At a leisurely pace, the rattler tracks down and inspects its kill. Then, it grabs the dead mammal's snout and begins swallowing, a process that an adult snake can complete within two minutes—a smaller snake may require a half hour or so to complete the process (Puskar 1994, personal communication).

Rattlers will also ambush prey at burrow entrances. Birds, bird eggs, and amphibians are also taken; upon striking birds, rattlers will instinctively hold on until the venom does its work. (Back at the basking areas, the gravid females do not hunt for prey from late June to birthing time in late August or early September. They draw on stored reserves while maintaining proper temperatures, assuring development of the eggs they carry.)

Mating occurs during July and August when males actively pursue the scent trails of potential mates. (The females can be sexually mature at age five or six—about thirty inches.) Although mating generally takes place on the summer foraging range, some mating activity seems to occur near the den. I suspect that some nongravid, sexually mature females never leave the denning-basking areas; at least, they may return to those areas to meet a mate, after doing some earlier foraging. On July 16, 1990, I was standing next to two medium-sized rattlers (females, I suspect) that were peacefully basking on top of a large, flat, den rock. Two four-foot snakes (males, I presume), identical in appearance, shot from beneath the den rock. (The fellow with me, on his first snake hunt, screamed—he scared the daylights out of me.) Their necks were intertwined as they muscled each other from side to side—a form of combat dance, I guess. Without thinking clearly (I should have backed off in order to observe), I picked the smaller snakes up and shuffled them under the rock to get them out of my way. The two males separated, one of them racing straight away into the laurel. I slipped my snake stick under the remaining male, which was still poised for battle. The snake remained tense, holding its configuration as I placed it on top of the den rock. It seemed oblivious to my presence, as if my snake stick was the new challenger. When I released it, it began patrolling the surface of the rock, concentrating on the spot where the females had lain, then "sniffing" all around the perimeter. The other male, also unconcerned with my potential threat, quickly returned to the rock. It would not climb up, but rested its head on one corner in order to watch its rival. When I left, the one was still watching the other trying to locate the nonexistent scent trail of the vanishing females.

Upon mating, the female timber rattlesnake stores the sperm, which fertilizes the eggs the following spring. At maximum, she could produce a brood every other year—normally several years elapse. The average litter size is eight (Allan Puskar captured a gravid female in Tioga County that gave birth to eighteen healthy young while in captivity). The infants, eight to twelve inches in length, are on their own. Often the entire litter lies intertwined at the basking rock well into September. Under normal birthing and weather conditions, the newborns will shed their skins a week or two after birth, then attempt to secure a meal before hibernation. The infants are quite capable of hunting small mammals (Reinert 1992, personal communication). But, reportedly, it is not critical that they feed before entering hibernation, for they can survive into the following season on an empty stomach. Soon, if they are to live, the infants must follow the scent trail of an older rattler to the winter quarters, a cavity they will probably use for life.

Longevity reports suggest that timber rattlesnakes may live to over thirty years in the wild; however, mortality rates during their first few years are high. One of the litter of eight may reach the age of four. The others will fall victim to the elements, starvation, parasites, and predation. In addition to the previously mentioned predators (humans, hawks, foxes), rattlesnakes have been killed and eaten by skunks and coyotes; deer and wild turkeys will kill rattlers. Individual sheep, pigs, dogs, and cats have also been known as proficient rattlesnake killers.

6

They Have a Friend
in Pennsylvania

I N   T H E   M I D - S I X T I E S ,   Y O U N G   H O W I E   R E I N E R T   C O U L D
be seen pedaling furiously, hurrying to his favorite snake-
hunting grounds on the outskirts of West Reading. He wasn't
afraid of snakes—his big brothers had handed him snakes when
he was a toddler—he was fascinated by them. During his teen
years, his hobby of hunting and capturing snakes turned into a
passion for studying snakes; he was marking water snakes, trying to make population estimates; he was Howard K. Reinert,
"junior biologist."

After earning his bachelor's degree in biology at Penn State in
1974, Reinert was employed by a Reading laboratory to prepare
environmental impact assessments on various pesticides and
other contaminants. But there were still snakes out there; and
some species were diminishing. They needed a spokesman—
and he'd have to be that person. In 1976, he entered graduate
school at Clarion University where he wrote his master's thesis
on the ecology and morphological variation of the massasauga
rattlesnake. Later, at Lehigh University, he received his Ph.D. in
biology. His dissertation concerned habitat variation within and
between sympatric snake populations—those of timber rattlesnakes and copperheads.

Reinert has held teaching positions at four Pennsylvania uni-
versities. Currently he is an assistant professor of ecology at
Trenton State College, but he also continues to serve as one of
Pennsylvania's leading authorities on the timber rattlesnake. He
is still pedaling furiously, trying to beat a deadline. He knows

how fast the timber rattler's domain is shrinking in the Northeast; he knows that, at the going rate, it's only a matter of time before the species vanishes.

Tracking Rattlers

Many of Reinert's timber rattlesnake studies involved the use of radiotelemetry for tracking subjects. In order to achieve a high degree of accuracy, he needed to develop a reliable procedure for installing transmitters; the goal was to obtain maximum trouble-free tracking with minimum change in the subject's behavior. Previous methods were inappropriate for scientific research because they affected the snake's ability to feed, move, or behave normally in general. (One of those methods was to force the transmitter down the snake's esophagus, then apply an external constricting band to prevent it being regurgitated.) Attempts to attach transmitters to the snake's exterior had poor results. Several researchers implanted transmitters surgically, but without antennas (the details of the implantation procedure were not published).

In 1982 Reinert and David Cundall published an article in *Copeia* entitled, "An Improved Surgical Implantation Method for Radio-Tracking Snakes." In it they describe implanting a transmitter assembly into a snake's body cavity at a point approximately three-fourths the snout to vent length behind the head. The transmitter was inserted through a half-inch incision made in the lower flank of the anesthetized snake; then the whip antenna was threaded under the skin, toward the snake's head. Transmitter weight varied from one-eighth to one-half ounce (depending on the type used), including the 1.4 volt mercury battery, twelve- to sixteen-inch antenna, and paraffin-beeswax coating.

Reinert and Cundall performed the fifteen-minute procedure fifty-five times on thirty-eight snakes during a two-year period with no cases of infection or mortality related to the operation. With the antenna advantage, transmitter range approached a mile across flat, wooded terrain. Through minor follow-up surgery, batteries were replaced at four- to ten-month intervals. Best of all, the snakes could travel and feed normally—six "wired," gravid rattlers produced broods. (Some of the snakes carried transmitters for nine years without any health problems, according to a follow-up report in 1990.)

The use of radiotelemetry in snake research has proved far superior to the old, traditional "random surveys" and "mark and recapture" methods. Since the 1970 advent of radio-tracking in snake research, many previously accepted "facts" about snake behavior and the habitats they use have been overturned. By utilizing the suggested components and implantation procedures of Reinert and Cundall, researchers are able to "gently" monitor a greater number and variety of specimens for longer periods, which further reduces bias in study results.

Beyond tracking, rapidly evolving medical and technological advances are providing research biologists with new opportunities to study intricate details of wildlife physiology under natural conditions. The new generation of research herpetologists can use radiotelemetry to monitor a free-roaming snake's temperature, heart rate, blood pressure, neuromuscular activity, and more. According to Reinert: "During the past two decades, telemetric studies have contributed significantly to our understanding of snakes. Undoubtedly, much of what will be learned during the next two decades will also be directly attributable to the use of this technology" (Reinert 1992, 195).

Habitat

From May 1979 through October 1981 (three "snake seasons"), Reinert headed a study designed to determine variation in habitat utilized by northern copperheads and timber rattlesnakes outside the winter den. This scientific study was the first

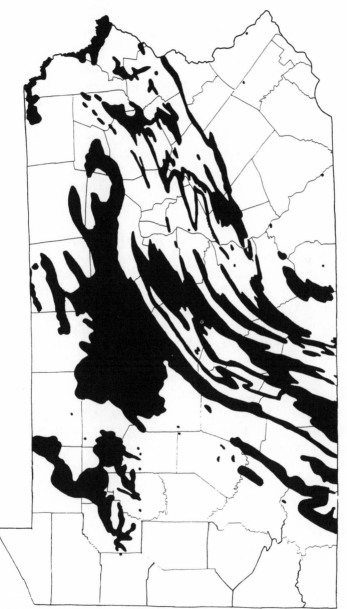

RANGE OF TIMBER RATTLESNAKE IN PENNSYLVANIA, 1994, *Courtesy W. H. Martin.*

in the world of herpetology to use radiotelemetry to determine habitat partitioning between and within species of snakes sharing the same locale. The study area, on a ridge in northern Berks County, Pennsylvania, encompassed a thousand acres of the Hawk Mountain Wildlife Sanctuary and surrounding state lands at an elevation of 590 feet to 1640 feet. Within the study area, this ridge, the leading ridge of Pennsylvania's Appalachian Mountain Section, is covered by a second-growth, mixed-oak stand comprised mainly of chestnut oak, red oak, black birch, and red maple. Ten percent of the area is classified as "forest openings," being either sandstone outcroppings or blueberry openings.

Reinert implanted transmitters in twenty-one timber rattlesnakes (twelve males, nine females; eleven black phase, ten yellow) and twenty northern copperheads. He limited subjects to adults since he surmised that the weight of the transmitters, even though only about a quarter-ounce each, could affect the behavior of smaller specimens. The average range of the transmitters under the study's conditions was 550 yards. Reinert observed each snake during every forty-eight-hour period for a minimum of three months, and some for sixteen months during the three-season study. When he located the subject in a stationary position (725 observations), as opposed to traveling, he recorded thirty-eight items relating to the structural habitat and climate of that location. Climatic variables included relative humidity and soil, surface, and air temperatures. Variables of habitat structure were rocks, leaves, low vegetation, logs, and trees; measurements of structure included length, height, diameter, percent coverage, stocking density, canopy closure, and distance-to. To prevent disturbing the subject snake, Reinert marked the location, then returned to collect some of the information when the snake had moved on. These methods enabled him to compare (1) habitat preference differences between the copperheads and rattlesnakes; (2) habitat preference differences between gravid female (carrying fertilized eggs), nongravid female, and male timber rattlesnakes; (3) habitat preference of light (yellow) versus dark (black) phase timber rattlesnakes.

Reinert published the results of his study in 1984 in *Ecology*. He revealed that, although timber rattlesnakes and copperheads share the same macrohabitat throughout our eastern temperate deciduous forest, niche preferences between them are significantly different; and niche preferences among timber rattlesnakes vary considerably depending on the snakes' sex and reproductive state—and noticeably between the color phases.

In general, the copperheads preferred open areas. At one end of that species' spectrum, gravid females were most apt to frequent very rocky sites that were virtually free of surface vegetation (low shrubs) or an overhead canopy; at the other end, male copperheads frequented areas characterized by moderately stocked young forest stands (44 percent canopy closure) having a generous amount of rocks and little surface vegetation. In contrast, timber rattlesnakes preferred older, more densely stocked timber stands having a significant cover of surface vegetation and fewer rocks. Gravid rattlers frequented very rocky sites having a sparse overhead canopy and a 25 percent cover of surface vegetation (compared to gravid copperheads' 2 percent).

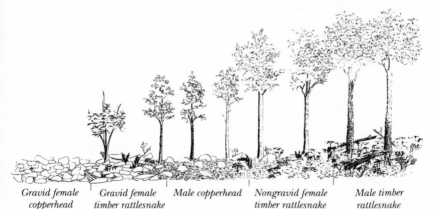

| Gravid female copperhead | Gravid female timber rattlesnake | Male copperhead | Nongravid female timber rattlesnake | Male timber rattlesnake |

PREFERRED HABITAT OF ADULT SNAKES ON THEIR SUMMER RANGE IN HOWARD REINERT'S STUDY AREA, BERKS COUNTY, PENNSYLVANIA.

At the opposite end of the rattler spectrum, males preferred a mature timber stand having a closed canopy, a dense carpet of surface vegetation, a supply of fallen logs, and few rocks. Nongravid timber rattlers preferred the near-closed canopy forest, but with less surface vegetation and more rocks than the male niche.

The habitat-selection-by-color-phase portion of Reinert's study centered on the male and nongravid rattlers. He discovered that the yellow phase snakes were associated more with pole-timber stands where stems were closer, leaf litter was heavier, and fallen logs were scarce, in comparison with the black phases' preference for bigger timber where stems had greater spacing and downed snags were more abundant. He linked this difference to the importance of background color matching for this species, which relies primarily on ambushing its prey.

Previous studies indicate that habitat separation between, and variation within, species may serve the ecological or evolutionary need to reduce competition. Other research shows that these differences can also occur when species evolve free of competition. Reinert believes that his study results are consistent with the competition theory, but that inherent physiological differences may be equally responsible in niche selection. The structure of habitat (such as canopy closure, percentage of rock, low shrubs) that a snake chooses is a primary factor in influencing the site's microclimate—temperature being of primary concern. Gravid snakes prefer higher body temperatures than their counterparts, and the female's temperature is a major factor in embryonic development. Reinert found that timber rattlesnakes were adaptable to, or would use a variety of sites within the required general habitat, but suggests that rocky, open areas may be *required* for successful reproduction—the gravid rattlers sought out this specialized habitat to fulfill their need for higher, and perhaps more stable, body temperatures. The nongravid females' preference for warmer habitat than the males', indicated by structure chosen, may be linked to heat requirements for egg formation during their nonreproductive years, according to Reinert.

Traditional texts describe the timber rattlesnake's preferred habitat as open, rocky areas. This was based on many years of observations by reputable biologists and naturalists. Using radio-telemetry, Reinert discovered that certain segments of the rattler community frequent rocky openings at various times during the season (April to October); there they are easily spotted by observers. The largest part of the colony, however, spends most of the season in the thick of the forest; the snakes often lie motionless as they wait for prey, and the observer passes by, none the wiser.

Foraging

Concurrent with his habitat utilization study on Hawk Mountain, Reinert, joined by David Cundall and Lauretta M. Bushar, studied the "Foraging Behavior of the Timber Rattlesnake in the Field" (published in *Copeia* in 1984). Because of the snake's secretive, low-profile nature on its home turf, most previous studies of feeding behavior had been conducted under laboratory conditions. Reinert's team kept tabs on twenty-one implanted specimens, at least once every forty-eight hours, for a total of 520 observations. In addition, they singled out one of the adult males and a gravid female for six twenty-four-hour vigils each. The study's findings strongly support suggestions by previous field researchers, who were relying on a very limited number of observations, that timber rattlers are primarily ambush predators: they secure most of their prey by patiently waiting beside rodent trails.

On the study area, a snake would take a typical ambush position adjacent to a fallen log. It would coil on the forest floor and, snug against the log, rest its lower jaw on the side of the log— poised to strike a rodent traveling the "balance beam" runway. (This should be known as the "Reinert Posture.") The researchers discovered male and nongravid rattlers in this posture about half the time they were relocated (197 of 418 observations). Consistent with the belief that gravid rattlers feed rarely, if ever, Reinert's team never discovered a gravid specimen in the ambush position after 102 observations.

In a related study, Douglass and Reinert showed that the upper surfaces of fallen logs are major travel routes for white-footed mice and other small mammals. Of 225 randomly sampled logs, 75 percent were used as runways at least once a day. Reinert believes that a rattler could forage effectively by staking out almost any downed snag. However, during the six day-long stints with the male rattler, he discovered that the snake would spend time snooping (smelling) around in an apparent effort to locate a "hot" log. Upon choosing a log, the

REINERT POSTURE

snake would tuck in for an average stay of over seven hours. Ambush behavior peaked between 9:00 P.M. and 8:00 A.M. During the 144 observation hours, the male spent 40 percent of its time in the ambush pose; 30 percent of its time exposed but inactive; 15 percent traveling; and 15 percent concealed. In contrast, the gravid female was concealed for 75 percent of the time; exposed but inactive for 20 percent; and traveling for the remainder.

Scat samples revealed that 65 percent of the prey taken were white-footed mice. The remainder consisted of red-backed voles, a chipmunk, a young rabbit, and a small bird. By comparing these percentages with the results of a previous survey of small mammals in the study area, Reinert believes that the timber rattler's mixed bag of prey species is directly proportional to the prey's occurrence.

Movements

During three activity seasons, from 1983 to 1985, Reinert, along with Robert T. Zappalorti, studied the movement patterns and habitat preference of timber rattlesnakes in the Pine Barrens of southern New Jersey. Again he used radiotelemetry to track six nongravid, seven gravid, and seven male snakes during the three-year period. The results were published in *Copeia* in 1988.

The habitat choices of the Pine Barrens snakes were similar to Reinert's earlier findings in Pennsylvania: the gravid females frequented open-canopy areas (along sand roads in this case), temperature being their first priority; the others headed into the thick cover for better foraging. But on this coastal plain, where there were fewer rocky openings and the small mammals had different habits, the role of fallen logs was reversed: in the Pennsylvania study, the use of fallen logs was associated with males, nongravid females, and foraging; in the Pine Barrens, gravid females sought fallen logs for temperature control and protection from predators. Since the prey species there seldom use the tops of the logs as runways, the foraging rattlers waited next to burrows, stump holes, and forest floor runways.

In the Pine Barrens, the summer range of an individual male timber rattler can be generally described as an oval area approximately one and three-quarters miles long and one mile wide, encompassing roughly one thousand acres of forestland. The snake leaves its den area, usually by the end of May, and sets off on a seemingly calculated, looping pattern of travel that will bring it home a week or two prior to hibernation. During the first month of dispersal, it appears to move apprehensively from its den area, traveling one hundred yards or so, then foraging on a small plot for several days before moving a short distance farther. By July, the male has reached its preferred activity area, perhaps a half mile or more from its den. Here it concentrates its foraging throughout a forty-acre plot over a period of several weeks or more. With the approach of the mating season (August in the Pine Barrens), the male may suddenly break its pattern to head for a new activity area where he has successfully located receptive females in the past. After tracking down a female and courting her for a while, he may race off to another prospective courting area, perhaps half a mile distant, where he'll search through a five- or ten-acre plot. By September, the male rattler is using an activity area that is close to his den for both foraging and late mating.

The typical nongravid female's summer range in the study area is similar to the male's; however, it is only about three-fourths the size. As in the male's case, the female's loop pattern is interrupted when she selects an activity area, where she may spend a month foraging throughout a ten- or twenty-acre tract (a smaller activity area than the male's). Later, she'll move on to an entirely new plot. Altogether, she may establish four or five of these separate major activity areas within her range during the season. The nongravid female continues this pattern even through mating season and lets the male find her. Reinert believes that the female's more conservative movement is related to her need to restore reserves lost during a previous season's pregnancy and to begin rebuilding for another.

By early June in this southern New Jersey study area, the typical gravid female leaves the den area and establishes a sixty-acre summer range located about a quarter mile away (because of the absence of closer, suitable basking habitat.) Throughout her chosen range, the pregnant rattler uses openings in small activity areas, which she changes gradually in an overlapping fashion during the course of the season. About a week after birthing, in late August, she returns to the den area via the same course she exited. For the month remaining prior to hibernation she forages within a small acreage.

By tracking the same snakes during two seasons, Reinert and Zappalorti discovered that an individual timber rattler generally uses the same dispersal route and activity areas it has become accustomed to—perhaps expanding the use of its range gradually over the years. Based on his earlier observations on Hawk Mountain, Reinert believes that the range size and movement patterns of Pennsylvania timber rattlesnakes parallel those of the Pine Barrens snakes, allowing for local topography and habitat configuration.

Climbing Ability

As a "novice timber rattler tracker" in 1979, Howard Reinert, with an antenna in his hand and a transmitter screaming away, circled a birch tree for twenty minutes; he was looking for a hole in the ground—or anything that the snake could be hiding under. Reaching for his note pad, he was prepared to write: "Timber rattlesnakes dig holes, enter, then seal the entrance behind," when he glanced toward the heavens for help; perched fifteen feet up the tree, the female rattler he'd been tracking returned his glance (and saved his career). The birch tree was six or seven inches in diameter, and the first limb was farther from the ground than the snake was long. A day or so later, the same snake was perched atop a six-foot stub; apparently it crawled up the still-attached, ramplike, fallen snag.

Since that episode, Reinert has discovered a half-dozen "climbers"; but they were mostly in shrubs and trees having limbs close to the ground or to adjacent shrub "bridges." One gravid female (the "heavenly serpent" from the previous year) climbed a Virginia creeper that shrouded a standing hemlock snag twelve inches in diameter; then it crawled out on a six-inch diameter limb—the resulting position was fifteen feet above a rockslide. And Reinert's assistant watched a large male rattler wander throughout the crown of a bushy white pine—until a limb snapped, that is.

Most terrestrial vipers are ill-equipped for climbing, in part due to the design of their circulatory system: when their heads are higher than their tails for very long, they faint. However, one of Reinert's colleagues, who is doing research on cardio-vascular control in snakes, told him that the timber rattlesnake's system is better suited for climbing than other species of rattlers.

Except for the gravid female, Reinert surmises that climbing rattlers may be following the scent trails of small mammals that are nesting or foraging in the shrubs and trees. It is also possible that they are thermoregulating (Reinert 1992, personal communication).

Organized Hunts

At the typical organized snake hunt in Pennsylvania, hunters pay a small registration fee so they can enter their catch as official competition participants. The registrants normally hunt individually or with a few friends; at some hunts guides are available to novices or hunters who are unfamiliar with the area. Registration usually begins at 8:00 A.M. Registered hunters may enter snakes for competitions in size, number of rattles, youngest hunter, ladies class, and so forth, until 5:00 P.M. Some hunts' rules require that entries be captured during a specified time period. Officials inspect the entries, occasionally rejecting snakes they deem "old catches" (captured days preceding the hunt).

Throughout the day, spectators watch successful hunters reveal their catch at the "pit"—a twenty-foot-square enclosure with a fence to keep onlookers at bay; inside is a smaller screened holding pen where the entered snakes are displayed. Snakes are measured by hunt officials, who straighten them against a ruler-board mounted on a table; then they're numbered with a marking pen, to be returned to their captors following the awards ceremony at five o'clock. (Today snakes cannot be sold, as was the past practice at some hunts.) A pit official is always "walking" a rattler throughout the arena, giving the audience a closer look and answering questions. Elsewhere on the grounds patrons may browse through a flea market, watch a ball game, sit down to barbecued chicken, or be treated to live music. The hunts have toned down a bit from the days when state troopers had to blast their cruisers through beer-can barricades in order to apprehend streakers who were dodging through an informal drag race (a.k.a. demolition derby) on the nearby highway.

From 1985 through 1987, Howard Reinert, contracted by the Pennsylvania Fish Commission with a grant from the Wild Resource Conservation Fund, conducted surveys at thirteen organized rattlesnake hunts in Pennsylvania: Morris (Tioga County, three times); Sinnemahoning (Cameron County, twice); Lock Haven (Clinton County, twice); Cresson (Blair County, once); Monroeton (Bradford County, twice); Towanda (Bradford County, once); Landisburg (Perry County, once); and Reedsville (Mifflin County, once). Hunt sponsors were either a fire company, a reptile association, or a sportsmen's organization.

The commission's decision to initiate the survey was partially influenced by respected timber rattlesnake studies which reported decreasing distributions and population levels of the snake in the Northeast—reports that prompted Connecticut,

New York, New Jersey, Massachusetts, and Rhode Island (and recently, Ohio) to legislate full protection of the species. The agency also considered additional reports that Pennsylvania harbors the largest contiguous population of timber rattlers in the Northeast, but that it is facing rapid decline, largely as a result of organized snake hunts. The survey was designed to gather biological data from the captured snakes, characterize snake hunters and their motives, determine the effects of the hunt on the snakes, and assess the value of organized hunts for public education and wildlife management.

Reinert and his assistants, with the cooperation of the hunt sponsors, inspected each timber rattler entered, taking measurements and noting coloration, sex, reproductive state, molting condition, and injuries; a Fish Commission tag was affixed to the base of the rattle for future identification. They then interviewed the successful hunters (sixty-four at thirteen hunts) and asked them to complete questionnaires relating to the capture of the snakes and their interest in hunting rattlers.

Most of those interviewed were men. Their average age was thirty-four, and they considered themselves veteran snake hunters. The majority listed "fun and sport" as the primary motivation for their hobby. Some also mentioned "danger and excitement," "photography," "nature study," "exercise," "trophies," and "a cure for boredom." Other hobbies high on their lists were hunting, fishing, and camping. Nearly all said that they release most of the snakes they capture, and some reported that they try to stock new areas or replenish over-hunted dens. They hunted primarily in open, rocky habitat (denning-basking areas). Some of them found areas that had been "torn apart" by other snake hunters. Questionnaire responses showed that 20 percent of the snakes were captured upon displacement of rock or log cover.

Inspections of the rattlers revealed that 29 percent had been injured during their capture and subsequent handling; they had sustained shedding tears, lacerations, head and vertebral damage. One had already died—the cranium had been disarticulated from the vertebral column. Reinert realized that he would have to abandon the population study he had designed as part of his survey: some of the hunters would not allow their snakes to be tagged; others said they would probably remove the tags prior to releasing the snakes. Reinert knew that many of the injured snakes would perish before the next season, and he knew others would not be released on their home territory.

In 1988, Reinert submitted his report and recommendations to the Pennsylvania Fish Commission and the Wild Resource Conservation Fund. His study, the results, and his recommendations were outlined in the *Journal of the Pennsylvania Academy of Science* in 1990. In the article's conclusions, he states: "Hunting rattlesnakes offers a challenging and unusual outdoor activity for a small number of Pennsylvania residents. However, organized events add little to this experience, and their negative aspects far outweigh any positive psychological, sociological, or economic benefit they may impart to participants, spectators, or sponsors" (Reinert 1990, 142).

One of his recommendations was to prohibit organized snake hunts, for the following reasons: the events are not valuable to research since samples are biased and information gathered from some participants is suspect; hunt activities (capture, transport, measuring, display) result in a high rate of injury to the snakes; releasing the snakes at other than original capture locations may be detrimental to them and to the rattlers native to the release sites; capturing and handling pregnant rattlers (84 percent of the females examined) may be injurious to the snake's general population, considering the large and increasing number of organized hunts; the hunts provide marginal educational value, at best (much of the information relayed to the spectators by hunters and sponsors is misleading or inaccurate); the whole affair constitutes commercial exploitation of wildlife.

Suspecting that the Fish Commission would buckle under political pressure from the small, special interest groups that oppose any legislation to restrict or prohibit organized timber rattlesnake hunts in Pennsylvania, Reinert offered a package of recommendations as an alternative to banning organized hunts. Some of his suggestions were: to limit the number of events to four annually; to establish a hunting season (at the time, there was no closed season) to occur in July, when most of the snakes are dispersed and when fewer shedding-tear injuries would result because most of them are then in a post-molt condition; to prohibit the use of nooses and discourage pinning; to prohibit the measuring of snakes by stretching them against a board; to prohibit the disruption of ground cover while hunting snakes; to provide stricter monitoring and enforcement by Fish Commission personnel; to use qualified instructors to provide educational programs for hunters and spectators; to prohibit contests involving snake handling and pit shows designed to force aggressive reactions from the rattlers.

> Although substantial populations of the timber rattlesnake presently exist in certain regions, the pressures of commercial and recreational hunting, indiscriminate killing, and habitat loss will probably continue to erode existing populations and their geographic distribution. (Reinert 1990, 143)

Translocating Rattlers

In the field of wildlife conservation and management, accepted theories, tools, and methods change with the conditions, our knowledge, and "the times." When I was introduced to the great outdoors, in the mid-sixties, the Game Commission paid schoolboys to trap rabbits in residential areas for release into public hunting areas. And any predatory animal was fair game anytime—a bounty was paid on some. Both of those programs have since been abolished, along with others that were finally deemed ineffective or counterproductive at a time when a trend to consider the well-being of all species of wildlife and their role in our environment was evolving. Funds that would have been directed to a rabbit or pheasant stocking program thirty years ago may now be helping to reestablish a viable population of a species that preys on rabbits and pheasants.

Stocking animals is an expensive and tricky, sometimes risky, undertaking. There have been plenty of failures—where the animal either fails to establish itself or thrives so well that it wreaks havoc with its native counterpart or other species. But there is a faction among sportsmen, wildlife agencies, and the general public that perceives stocking as a quick fix for a variety of wildlife management problems.

Some rattlesnake hunters have been stocking timber rattlers for years, especially since the species began to decline noticeably. The hunters translocate the snakes—they take them from one denning area and release them at another. Sometimes they do this in an effort to reestablish the snake at a den that they believe has been cleaned out. Other times they are trying to stockpile snakes at their favorite den for some future use; or they may be trying to remove snakes from an area where they are being over-hunted or randomly killed in an effort to save them. Also, the sponsors of organized snake hunts have sometimes dumped their event's catch at denning areas previously unknown to the snakes. I use the phrases "in an effort to" and "trying to" because rarely, if ever, do hunters that translocate timber rattle-snakes ever see the snakes again.

All the snake hunters I know personally have translocated rattlers at least once, and some have repeatedly. *Most* of us have had enough sense not to put them in places where they have never historically existed; but beyond that, it's guess work. Realizing that this practice is relatively common and widespread, the Fish Commission asked Reinert to study the effects of translocating timber rattlers. They want to know how individual rattlers react when released into a different den-colony, what impact they have on the resident snakes, and how this practice could affect the species and its population level over a long term. And there may come a day when conservation employees are expected to remove nuisance snakes or move a colony from a site that is slated for development. What might be the effects of such a policy? Preliminary reports of this study, which may be ongoing, should be available in 1995.

Due to inconsistencies in the use of terminology among herpetologists in this relatively new and expanding research field, Reinert wrote an article in 1991 that attempts, in part, to standardize translocation terminology. He suggests that *translocation* covers all situations where organisms are moved from one place to another. Translocation may be employed for purposes of *repatriation* (releasing a species into an area that it formerly occupied), *introduction* (releasing a species into an area where it does not and has not naturally occurred), *reintroduction* (introduction in an area of previous, failed introduction), and *augmentation* (release of individuals of a species into an area already occupied by that species).

In this article, Reinert addresses the potential genetic risks in translocation, for example, "out-breeding depression," which involves the reduction of fitness of a population as a result of mixing naturally isolated colonies. And, outlining examples of captive breeding and release programs having undesirable side effects, he states: "the release of a large number of poorly adapted individuals into an existing, natural population could have a negative impact on the existing gene pool." He also discusses potential problems in the social behavior of translocated specimens and the native individuals in the area of translocation, further stating: "the topic of translocations suffers from a deficiency of sound scientific scrutiny and an inadequate understanding among legislators, government agencies, and the general public of its complexity and potential for success."

Reinert has plans to study the Aruba Island rattlesnake. I asked him if he'll still be working with Pennsylvania's timber rattler. He quickly replied, "You bet!"

7

Hunting Rattlers

ALL BONA FIDE TIMBER RATTLER HUNTERS ARE plagued by the most hideous of nightmares sometime during their careers. It may be within the first week, or several years later. Usually, the plague is short-lived, lasting only a year or two. I vividly recall a dream in which a forty-foot, van-type, tractor trailer was parked in my front lawn. I opened the trailer's doors to see what was inside—bad move. My daughter and my wife were standing in trepidation at the far end. Between us writhed a thousand rattlers that were acting like they weren't a bit impressed with the shock absorbers on the trip across Interstate 80. I realized that my snake stick, as if it would have made any difference, was in my truck, which I had lent to my brother-in-law for the day. It was a totally hopeless predicament. Fortunately I awoke before I was bitten, or I probably would have died of shock while I slept.

Before engaging in the sport of timber rattlesnake hunting, hunters must obtain a permit from the Pennsylvania Fish and Boat Commission. This is required if one intends to hunt for, capture, take, kill, or possess a timber rattler. The permit is inexpensive, intended to help the agency monitor the hunting pressure on this reptile.

The dangers to the rattlesnake hunter in the Northcentral Pennsylvania summer woods are not much greater than those threatening hikers, birders, and other forest users—except that rattlesnake hunters generally roam far from the trail, and they spend a greater amount of time on a more formidable walking surface. The common dangers and irritations that can be planned for include: nagging and stinging insects (allergic reaction, Lyme disease); sunburn; disorientation (panic, hypothermia); sprains; dehydration (heat cramp, heat stroke, exhaustion); bad water (intestinal disorders, giardiasis); poisonous plants; and, of course, poisonous snakes.

There was a time when the only thing I worried about was "how many snakes I might miss out on." There was no preparation; I entered the woods as did my fellow snake hunters—with reckless abandon. (Some of them were—or still are—equipped with a T-shirt, blue jeans, white socks, sneakers, a bag, and snake pincers—period). But today I think more about staying healthy so that I don't miss out on the next snake expedition. I wear a quality pair of eight- to ten-inch, leather, lace-up sportsmen's boots that are large enough to accommodate medium-weight socks over thin ones—wool over polypropylene is a smart choice. Heavyweight, loose-fitting blue jeans that are extra-long provide several safety benefits: they're not bad for busting through laurel and brambles; they deter insect pests; they've been known to deflect or "absorb" snake bite. I pull the trouser bottoms to the tops of the boots, then wrap them with duct tape—this allows for freedom of movement while repelling ticks and keeping debris out of my boots. I wear a long-sleeved cotton shirt when it's cool and when pesky insects are numerous; when it's shed, a double layer of T-shirt remains effective against those buggers that drill right through a single wet T-shirt. A baseball-style field cap shades the eyes while fending off the pursuing insects. In the summer woods, "dark and drab" is always fashionable—those bent on dressing brightly usually carry an extra bottle of insect repellent. A pair of UV-tinted eyeglasses is recommended safety gear on the rocky, sunny slopes.

Additional gear is added according to the intended length of the hunt or its distance from a regularly traveled road. I generally carry a topographic map and compass if I'm heading far from civilization, even in country I'm quite familiar with. I don't want to rely strictly on my recollection, especially knowing that it could be shaken by fog, darkness, or an emergency.

The simple act of drinking water is often postponed or overlooked as a necessity for a safe, enjoyable—and fulfilling—day afield. Having to stop and drink is considered by most as a sign of weakness. The fact is, when you *have to* stop and drink, you *are* getting weak—you've already lost "the edge." The dehydration process, or the body's reaction to possible dehydration, robs your stamina. The solution is to drink water—*not* sweet beverages or alcohol—before starting vigorous activity; force it into the tank. Then carry a quart canteen of water—throw in a quarter teaspoon of table salt—and sip regularly throughout the activity, before thirst indicates the need. If you work yourself into exhaustion and thirst, *then* stop to drink, you will not function to your full potential. *And*, if you press on without drinking, you're inviting trouble.

All of the mentioned accessories can be carried in a fanny pack. I usually throw in a bee-sting kit and matches. And I occasionally check with the area poison center for its current recommendations on field first aid for poisonous snakebite, but it is low on my list of concerns. I trust that a day will come when I realize that my senses, common sense, and coordination are eroding; I'll probably invest in snake-proof gaiters.

The rattlesnake hunter's most valuable safeguard is a hunting partner. In lieu of a pard, I leave a "game plan" on the kitchen table. Included is the name of a person who could (and would) track me down if need be. At the end of the note I write: "Donna, Don't panic until 2 hours after dark." When I return home, I see she's answered: "Don't worry Honey, I won't."

For capturing timber rattlers, I prefer the device introduced to me by Ray Low. It consists of a $5/16$-inch lag-thread, open-shanked ceiling hook screwed into the end of a ¾-inch by 3-foot hardwood dowel. A chunk of tubing or a hose clamp is secured on the end of the dowel prior to the drilling and screwing operation. The hook is opened up a bit beyond stock dimensions, and rough edges are filed—the end of the shank should be rounded. A 4-foot dowel is better suited if the catcher is to double as a walking stick. With the Ray Low stick, the hunter slips the hook under the rattler's belly at a point approximately one-third the snake's length behind its head, rotates the stick slightly, and quickly lifts the snake several feet into the air. The hunter has already eyed an open, flat spot for gently "landing" the snake if it tries to glide off the stick. Some snakes are very cooperative, while others get used to the balancing act only after several rides. A common mistake made by the novice is placing the hook over the top of the snake instead of beneath it. Another is failure to lift the snake high enough—if it thinks it can reach down to the ground or a shrub, it will try to. A third is to allow the snake to scoot off the stick and fall to the ground. (A rattlesnake can advance over any thin, suspended stem by powering ahead with its scutes, or belly scales. When it is over center, and there is nothing for its anterior to rest upon, it slips and falls.) Foreseeing this, the hunter should quickly lower the serpent, then re-hook it and lift again.

Many hunters prefer the professional-style, aluminum snake pincers—I have a pair but seldom use them. I suppose if grabbing a snake and not allowing any chance of its escape is the first priority, the pincers are superior to the hooked stick. However, if you grab the snake's midsection (in order to prevent injury to its neck), the rattler will often strike the pincer's metal shaft and break a fang (if not its mouth). Also, I believe these devices are responsible for the majority of the shedding-tear injuries that are so evident on snakes captured during organized hunts. These high-priced snake sticks are not necessary for handling timber rattlesnakes.

Hunters trying to make devices to capture rattlers alive have produced some real snake killers. I know one fellow who threaded a piece of wire through a four-foot length of copper tubing, forming a small loop at one end. Using this hand-operated snare, he attempted to catch a big yellow phase for a

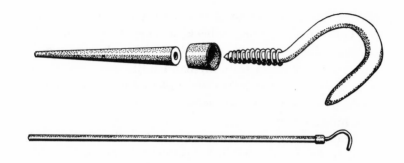

THE RAY LOW STICK

talk at scout camp. I'm not sure if it was the cutting and choking that killed the snake or if it broke its neck as it thrashed about. Another gadget I saw appeared quite impressive upon first glance—it had a trigger on the handle. But when you squeezed the trigger the gripping jaws would slam shut with enough force to crimp the steam pipe on a runaway locomotive. I'm sure there were no survivors.

Flailing at rattlers with a hooked stick, dragging them through the rocks and brush with pincers, pinning them with excessive pressure, pinning their heads and allowing them to thrash or wriggle, suspending them by the neck, and dropping them are all activities employed by novice and careless timber rattlesnake hunters. They needlessly—mostly unintentionally—injure and kill the snakes they capture and handle; they think this little reptile is much tougher than it actually is. As part of a three-year study, the snake ecologist Howard K. Reinert discovered that 29 percent of the rattlers he examined at organized snake hunts in Pennsylvania had *visible* injuries. Shedding tears were high on the list; snakes are most susceptible to this injury during the three weeks prior to shedding. A tear in the outer skin can result in deformation of the underlying layer; also, it allows fungus and bacteria to invade the new, still unseasoned, underlying skin. Reinert also observed snakes with internal head injuries and major lacerations on the neck and body. One snake was dead; its cranium had been disarticulated from the vertebral column. "Such an injury may occur when a snake that is pinned or held by the head thrashes violently. Disarticulation could also be a consequence of measuring snakes by stretching them along a straight ruler" (Reinert 1990, 139). Prying a snake's mouth open to display its fangs, excessive head-pinning pressure, and causing a snake to bite or strike at a hard object can all cause damage to its fangs, teeth, and mouth lining and may result in a condition known as mouth rot. In some instances, this condition eventually causes death.

Hunters normally transport live timber rattlesnakes in a cloth sack. Coarse-weave feed bags and pillowcases were commonly used by the ridgerunners during the heyday of the organized hunts; but a heavier, fine-weave cotton sack with minimum dimensions of thirty-two inches deep by twenty inches wide is better suited. Methods to get the snake in the sack are almost as numerous as the hunters themselves—and most don't warrant mention. Hunter safety and the well-being of the animal will take precedence in the actions of the responsible hunter. A snake bag that has three stout, eighteen-inch cords firmly attached to its opening edge is a suitable choice—opposing pulls form a triangular opening. A fiasco-free transfer from the hooked stick to the bag is accomplished by using trees or comrades as props to hold the bag open. Some rattlers will dodge the opening and wind up crawling on top of the sack and outstretched cords. It must be relifted and held above the opening. As soon as it lowers its anterior, it should be quickly maneuvered into the sack.

Rattlers often successfully "stand up" against the sack's interior in an effort to escape—once a rattler's head breaks over the edge, it's home free. To prevent this, the hunter, once the snake has been placed into the bag, grasps the top of the bag firmly with both hands and, holding the bag open in order to observe the snake, gently shakes the "climber" back down. Lightly touching the sack's bottom to the ground, the hunter quickly twists its top shut, forming a twelve- to fifteen-inch neck or handle; a piece of cord is used to tie the handle low (near the snake) and high. Only careless hunters allow the sack's "snake compartment" to contact their bodies—there have been enough fang-through-the-bag incidents to serve fair warning. In addition to cloth sacks, hunters use a variety of containers to carry rattlers from the woods, including hoop-net-type sacks and wooden boxes. Some attach a small wooden box to a packboard. The thought of sledding down a rockslide on a disintegrating box full of pit vipers that are seeing double always deterred me from experimenting with that method.

I use a fifteen-gallon plastic drum with a screw cap—a mushroom container—as a temporary holding box when I'm keeping a rattler for a training program. These lightweight, rugged jugs are inexpensive and easy to clean. Vent holes can be drilled and a locking hasp can be easily installed—I worry about curious youngsters. Any holding box should be kept in a shady, well-ventilated, cool environment (less than eighty degrees Fahrenheit). Even a vented container will "bake" a snake in short order if it is placed in the sun or left in a closed shed or vehicle on a hot day. Numerous physiological complications *will* develop in a snake that is improperly cared for. Persons desiring to hold a rattler in captivity for more than several days should consult an expert.

For the sake of both the handler and the snake, a squeeze box should be used when examining, marking, sexing, and measuring timber rattlers. A rattler held and "stretched" for measurement by the traditional organized snake hunt standard can break its neck as it strains to muscle its way out of the predicament. Using the squeeze box method, a wheeled map measurer is run on the plexiglas used to press the snake into foam rubber. (Howard Reinert [1990] suggested to the Fish Commission that this be included in the regulations.) A thin wire cable and a tape measure will suffice in lieu of a map measurer. Officials of organized snake hunts should use this method when measuring for the "longest" contest, especially since many of the snakes are now returned to their captors who release them. In the event of a potential record breaker, the traditional method of measuring could also be used, with both lengths recorded for future reference. (Length measured in a squeeze box may be an inch or two shorter for a mid-forties-inch rattler.)

No fail-proof method is known for determining a timber rattler's sex by visually inspecting external features. The male's tail is generally longer, but there is a gray zone on the comparison charts: females normally have thirteen to twenty-four subcaudal scales (underside, cloaca to rattle); males have twenty to thirty. The female's body often rounds off bluntly at the cloaca, the adjoining tail becoming distinctly smaller in diameter; that area of a male is often more gracefully tapered. In Pennsylvania, licensed rattlesnake hunters are required to supply an annual report concerning the snakes they've captured; the report is to include the sex of each snake. The Fish Commission provides instructions for probing a snake to determine its sex. The rattlesnake's sex can be determined with the aid of a squeeze box, a

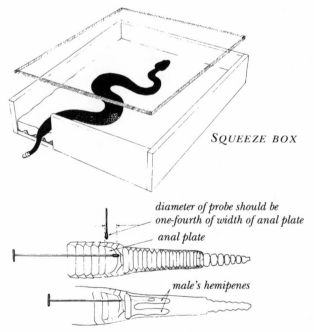

SQUEEZE BOX

diameter of probe should be one-fourth of width of anal plate

anal plate

male's hemipenes

PROBING (to determine sex)

helper, and a one-sixteenth-inch diameter blunt-tipped rod which has been lightly lubricated with vaseline. A rounded plastic cotton swab shaft could be used on an adult snake. (Also, reptile supply houses sell sexing probes.) The probe's diameter should not exceed one-fourth the anal plate width measured along the snake's midline. The probe is slowly rotated as it is gently inserted into the cloaca, near one side, and pushed toward the rattle. The probe will enter to a point eight to sixteen subcaudal scales from the cloaca entrance in a male, one to three in a female.

I don't recommend probing rattlers unless the hunter intends to harvest one and, being conservation minded, would like to select a male. Otherwise, there's no sense running amuck in the Northcentral wilds handling and probing the serpents to gather statistics that have already been collected by qualified biologists, especially since those biologists have stated that improper or excessive handling is detrimental to the snakes.

Experienced and considerate timber rattlesnake hunters employ restraint in their hunting methods in addition to abiding by the Fish Commission's regulations. They are concerned about the species' status and the future of the hobby—they enjoy a quality hunt. They do not flip, slide, or otherwise haul rocks or logs when trying to locate or capture rattlers; if the snakes are "down," these hunters write it off as a bad day to hunt and make plans to return. When they handle a snake, they realize that they are holding a fragile creation; if it is frantically winding its way through the brush or trying to squeeze into a crevice, they let it escape—on the right day, it'll be out in the open and lethargic. When smart hunters release rattlers, it is at the point of capture; otherwise the snakes will probably never be seen again. Snake ecologists suspect that a displaced timber rattlesnake spends the remainder of the activity season trying to find its home territory, and some will freeze to death rather than associate with a colony of strangers.

Regulations

The Pennsylvania Fish and Boat Commission is charged, in part, with the management of the commonwealth's reptiles and amphibians. Since 1979, the timber rattlesnake has enjoyed some form of protection as spelled out in part II of the *Fishing and Boating Regulations,* published annually by the commission.

Chapter 75 discusses fish, reptiles, and amphibians that are "endangered," "threatened," and "candidates." Endangered and threatened species have full protection—there are no open seasons during which they may be legally pursued, captured, or killed. Candidate species are those that can be legally harvested according to special regulations (methods, seasons, limits, permits) but are being watched closely; they may be in line for redesignation, up or down. People are encouraged to release candidate species "immediately and unharmed to the waters or other area from which they were taken." The timber rattlesnake, *Crotalus horridus,* is listed as a candidate species.

Chapter 77 covers specific regulations pertaining to timber rattlesnakes. The following general summary is current for 1994 only. Specific questions should be directed to the commission's herpetology and endangered species coordinator.

Permit Required

A person who hunts (pursues in an effort to capture or kill) timber rattlesnakes in Pennsylvania must have an Individual Rattlesnake Hunter Permit in his (or her) possession while hunting for, taking, capturing, killing, or possessing a timber rattlesnake. The fee for the annual permit is $5.00. Specific instructions with the permit require the permittee to file a report concerning his snake hunting activity by November 1 of the permit year, even if he didn't hunt or capture any rattlers. Failure to do so could result in a rejection of the next application. The "Application for Individual Rattlesnake Hunter Permit" is available from: Herpetology and Endangered Species Coordinator, Bureau of Fisheries, 450 Robinson Lane, Bellefonte, Pa. 16823-9620.

An individual who is not hunting timber rattlesnakes and does not have a permit, yet kills a timber rattler, can legally do so if he believes he acted under a reasonable apprehension of immediate death or bodily harm to himself or other persons in his immediate vicinity. If he kills more than one per day, or if he has more than one in his possession and he intends to use the mentioned "defense" if questioned by a law officer, he must notify the commission in writing at the above address within five business days following the kill.

Season, Limits

The legal season for hunting timber rattlesnakes (pursuing with intent to capture or kill) is: "Second Saturday in June to July 31."

The daily limit is one. The possession limit is one. During the closed season, the possession limit is one.

Additional

When hunting timber rattlesnakes it is prohibited to use chemicals, smoke, explosives, winches, auto jacks, or other devices or materials that could damage or destroy a den or its surroundings.

It is unlawful to sell or attempt to sell a timber rattlesnake or any part of one.

Certain natural areas in the state forests are posted against the hunting, capturing, killing, or possessing of any reptile or amphibian.

Organized Hunts

Specific legislation defines "organized snake hunts." In general, if a person or organization intends to sponsor an organized hunt, they must submit an application to the herpetology and endangered species coordinator between January 1 and March 1 of the year of the proposed event. An issued permit fee is $25.00. The commission reserves the right to deny a permit if it feels the sponsor is not qualified to conduct the event in the specified manner or if another permit for a hunt to occur within the same general area and within four weeks has been issued.

Free handling (holding the snake in the hand in a manner whereby the snake's head is free to bite or strike) of timber rattlers or any other venomous reptiles is prohibited at organized events. Sacking contests (a competition wherein participants place rattlers in a bag or container in a timed event) using timber rattlers is prohibited. Other species of rattlers not native to Pennsylvania may be used if they were procured legally.

Snakes may not be confined without water or shade or otherwise abused or handled roughly.

At the conclusion of an organized snake hunt, the timber rattlers must be released unharmed into the area from which they were taken. (Most sponsors mark the snakes and return them to their captors who are supposed to release them into the area of capture.)

Additional requirements of organized hunt sponsors are specified with the issued permit.

8

The Really Dangerous Ones

WHEN GARY DILLMAN AND I SEIZED OUR MOMENT in the local spotlight at the Morris Hunt in 1977, we didn't realize that our names and mugs, although reversed, would wind up in a future issue of *Strength & Health*, a weight lifters' magazine published in York, Pennsylvania; but eleven months afterward, I received a bizarre, anonymously scribbled letter, which had been postmarked in Yonkers, New York. It mentioned that my photo was in the magazine's May 1978 issue, clipping attached. It further stated that I was as eloquent looking as "so and so's" sculpture of a reclining female nude, photo clipping also enclosed. To this day I haven't determined if I was being attacked by a perverted animal rights activist or if one of my demented friends was cuing me to procure a copy of the issue. I suspect the latter since the sender centered Gary in the clipping while neatly cutting my face right down the middle.

After I frantically called a half-dozen bookstores, my relatives located a copy of the magazine in Williamsport. The article briefly mentioned the Morris Snake Hunt, telling how demanding a warm June rattlesnake hunt can be on one's body. It said that not only the legs need to be conditioned, but upper body strength was crucial due to the pack one would be toting all day. The article went on to describe a daily fitness routine for would-be snake hunters, mentioning exercises I'd never heard of: bench presses, half squats, straight arm pullovers, powercleans, and curls. I had a good laugh; I hadn't done so much as a push-up since high school gym class.

The way we used to hunt snakes, a person would have been nuts to carry a pack, let alone try to get in shape ahead of time. Heck no! We'd even scoff at someone who was foolish enough to carry a canteen. The object was to hunt two or three steep sidehills at a blazing pace, building a tremendous thirst, then lead-foot-it to the nearest "real" watering hole. Upon arrival at the therapeutic, air-conditioned retreat, we'd hash over the past several years' worth of snake hunting adventures—

the same old stories, over and over again. I, of course, was an unwilling participant in the fuddled behavior, cooperating only out of fear. The same fear dampens my desire to mention the worst of the atrocities committed by the snake hunting partners I'll be introducing shortly. Most of these ridgerunners carry large-bore hip irons; when they become the least bit bored, or if they want to get your attention, they've been known to fire at random.

Dillman is definitely dangerous, and it may be my fault. You see, on our first rattlesnake hunt together, we both had our snake sticks hooked on a very large chunk of shalerock we were trying to haul. We were standing shoulder to shoulder, straining every muscle from our toes to our ears, when my stick slipped, levered through the air, and struck Gary squarely in the nose. He dropped to his knees, hands clutching his face. When he came up for air, he showed me the blood on his hands. To this day, he claims I laughed uncontrollably as I raced ahead to the next rock outcropping, leaving him behind. If I remember right, I was crying, not laughing, and, thinking that I had inflicted a serious injury upon him, was running to summon an ambulance. Due to stress and fear, I became disoriented and ran toward a nearby ledge instead of our vehicle.

On another occasion Gary and I were hunting down on Young Womans Creek one afternoon. When we came off the hill, Gary dumped a black rattler from his bag so that we could take a closer look at it. Shortly, a car came down the road and stopped next to us; the snake lay motionless between us and the car. A gentleman in his fifties, sitting in the passenger seat, rolled down his window and, pointing to the nearby stream, asked, "Is that water safe to drink?"

Gary, pointing to the snake, replied, "Yeah, but you'd better watch out for these."

The man shrieked, "Oh my God! Where did you catch that thing!"

Gary, now on a roll, responded, "Over there, next to the crick."

The man asked, "How far can they jump?"

Gary answered "Oh, about five feet." Immediately, the car window shot halfway up.

The driver indicated he still intended to fill his thermos at the creek. A squabble ensued, when finally the passenger shouted, "Go ahead! Be a hero!" Not wanting to upset his friend, the driver proceeded down the road, probably en route to Renovo where a "safe" water source could be located. Dillman cackled wildly.

One last performance: Gary was driving his Scout pickup down the Baldwin Branch Road at what I still consider to be a high rate of speed for a single lane, gravel road. I was trying to coordinate the map with our road position in order to determine where we should stop to hunt a particular ridge. A bit nervous because of our rate of travel, I lost my concentration and foolishly indicated such. Dillman, muttering something about the day being half shot, plucked the map from my hands. As we continued on, I realized I was the only one watching the road and that we were accelerating. I screamed when I saw a flash of blue through the laurel that was blocking our view of a rapidly approaching curve. We slid uncontrollably, halting within several feet of a van that had been approaching in similar fashion. The van was unfamiliar to us. Before we could remaneuver to the edge of the road, two thugs sprang from the vehicle and trained their revolvers on Gary's radiator. We were very relieved when we recognized the two thugs as old snake-hunting buddies, Jimm Leach and Rawley Grant.

There's so much I can't write about Gary Dillman; to get a better picture, multiply what I've mentioned by three or so.

On my first rattlesnake hunt, the soft-spoken forest ranger Ray Low made a lasting impression on me. (I had heard stories from several sources about the rattler Ray transported loose in his Bronco one day when he forgot his snake box. By the time he arrived home, the snake had established residency in the mass of wires, cables, and shafts in the heart of the vehicle's dashboard. The removal process entailed major surgery.) When I arrived at Ray's residence, he offered to drive. Upon assuring me that his vehicle was serpent-free, we headed for parts unknown. Soon we were working our way up a steep rocky point. As he flipped through the rocks searching for a rat-tler, this wiry bantam was springing up, down, and sideways like a leprechaun with his shoe on fire. Here he was, eighteen years my senior and I couldn't come close to staying with him, let alone look for snakes. Near the crest of the hill, he found a rattler. He intended to carry it off the mountain on his snake stick, then he spied a piece of plastic flapping in the breeze—it was the remains of a shelter that a hunter had lashed to a clump of trees. Ray fabricated a bag of sorts, sealing the snake in a see-through bubble. He said we'd have to hurry to the vehicle or the snake would surely suffocate.

Our second hunting location that evening was an abandoned flagstone quarry about a hundred yards from a forestry road. It was getting dusky by the time we began picking through the old tailings. Ray was on the steep slope below the flat of the quarry; I was checking the heaps of scrap stone on the flat. After a short search, Ray hollered, "Box! Box! Fetch my box!" I rushed to the Bronco and grabbed the crudely constructed snake container. I dashed back along the quarry lane in the now dim light, with fogging glasses and perspiration further reducing visibility. While I trotted through the scattered sweet ferns on the flat, I could see that Ray was still hunched over, trying to extract the snake from its crevice. As I stopped, panting heavily, I simultaneously noticed a rattler striking at me from within several feet (I clearly recall the flash of white—the lining of its mouth—rocketing from the darkened ferns.) The resulting squeal seemed to echo off the quarry wall for twenty seconds. When I landed, five to eight feet away, I noticed Ray's beady eyes trained upon me. In his soft, high-pitched voice he half giggled, "Oh yeah, I forgot to tell you. I put three of 'em up there. Keep an eye on 'em 'til I get this other bugger." (From my observations of rattlers since that episode, I know that the snake had feigned the strike. Had I been standing on it when I decided to stop, it might not have feinted and I probably would have fainted.) I learned two things that evening: never run through ferns during the dim of night, and never expect a hard-core snake hunter to issue a warning as you semiconsciously approach a pit viper.

Ray was a guide for the annual Morris Hunt. Although I'm not one who enjoys hunting with a large gang for anything, I decided to join Ray's party that year. Upon arriving at the designated rendezvous, I had second thoughts. The first of Ray's "clients" I saw wore a silk shirt, gold necklace, and cowboy boots; he was so unfit that he had a hard time extracting himself from the bucket seat of his sports car. The next gentleman I met carried a snake-catching device he'd purchased from a peddler at the hunt head-quarters that morning. It was of a spring-loaded, cam-action design that unexpectedly and uncontrollably snaps shut to a one-size-crushes-all position. By midmorning I'd seen enough—and I didn't want to get stuck having to drag some weekend warrior out of the woods; I went my separate way.

Through the years, Ray and I hunted together only upon occasion; I would scold him repeatedly for guiding other hunters. We kept our favorite dens secret, often teasing each other about who knew the best spots. One day we were both hinting about a good den we'd found; the dens seemed to be in the same locality. I argued that I knew exactly where his den was; he claimed that I did not, but that he knew where mine was. Finally we made a deal. He'd show me his den—if it wasn't the one I'd been talking about, I'd have to show him mine. So on a bright July morning we headed across the Pine Creek Plateau toward a rock knoll, whereupon Ray showed me "his" den rock. I'd been there previously but considered it a fair revelation on his part. Being of occasionally honorable character, I led Ray a quarter-mile through the thicket to a superior den that was previously unknown to him. I threatened him with bodily harm if I ever discovered he'd revealed "my" den to anyone, but I knew the threat was useless.

The following year I inspected my "secret" den on the day after the Morris Hunt. I found a fresh two-foot section of Ray's now splintered snake stick; he'd tried to pry up my den rock—and he, no doubt, guided the crew to the scene. This meant war. This Low fellow is dangerous.

I met Al Puskar the summer he supervised a Youth Conservation Corps crew in the Wellsboro area—he'd asked me to present a timber rattlesnake program to his crew. Being an ecology teacher with a special interest in reptiles and amphibians, Al quickly fell in love with the rattler of the timber. His huge collection of turtles, frogs, snakes, and other scaled animals harbored

in the high school lab was lacking one thing—a venomous snake. Soon he was raising and studying timber rattlers. When Al wasn't picketing against some fast food joint that got caught mixing whale blubber into their fish sticks, he made a good snake-hunting partner. He started his own local campaign to save the timber rattler. He could write a heck of a letter to an agency or an editor or a politician—almost; he'd always lose it in the last paragraph, using phrases like "atrocious barbarian."

The year after finding Ray's broken snake stick at my favorite den, I made plans to retaliate. I suspected that Ray would return to the rock, with his crew, on the day of the Morris Hunt. I commandeered Puskar, along with my daughter, Tushanna. On Snake Hunt morning, our mission was to get to the Pine Plateau denning-basking area well before Ray and his gang arrived and frighten as many rattlers as we could find back into their dens. It was a perfect morning—the snakes were up and sunning early. We systematically and swiftly worked from ledge to ledge, scaring the dickens out of every rattler we spotted; it was a meticulously engineered plan. At one point, Shan and I stepped over a yellow rattler we hadn't seen. Al pointed it out and shuffled it into its crevice. When we reached the last ledge, we sat down for a rest; we were on top of the highest outcropping. Ray's group was not yet in sight, but if they followed the same route we had taken, the snakes, having had time to calm down, would be basking on the surface again. We decided to return to our starting point to rerun the routine, but just as we started to leave we heard a distant clattering of rocks. Soon we heard voices and the distinct clicking of snake sticks on the sandstone boulders. The crew was working its way up the mountainside, directly toward us. There was silence as the hunters paused for a breather thirty yards below our buzzard roost pinnacle; a dense canopy of brush obstructed our view. I made a loud comment concerning "rock haulers." There was no reply. I followed, "Must be Ray Low is down there!"

The reply—"Who's he? Never heard of anybody by that name"—came from the soft-spoken ridgerunner himself. We went down. Few words were exchanged. Ray said, "I know why you're here." I felt bad. Here I was, ruining a snake hunt for the friend that introduced me to the sport. Ray knew I was committed to helping bring the uncontrolled exploitation of timber rattlesnakes to a halt. He understood, although he didn't agree.

Several months later, with wounds healed and the previous episode far from my thoughts, I sat in my office doing paperwork. I heard the main office door open, followed by the familiar voice of Waterways Patrolman Ray Hoover who blurted, "Curt Brennan here?" Within seconds he stormed into my room with a letter clutched tightly in his hand. Waving it in front of my face he asked, "Who's this Al Puskar guy—some crackpot or what?"

I immediately replied, "Yes. What's going on?" Ray explained that Al had written the Fish Commission, saying that he and I knew of snake hunt officials violating the newly enacted law prohibiting the altering or damaging of rattlesnake dens. Hoover didn't think too much of rattlers to begin with, so having Harrisburg direct him to pounce on a couple of local yokels for flipping a few rocks had him steaming. Al wasn't trying to get anyone arrested, but he wanted the commission to step up its regulations and enforcement. I couldn't bear the thought of my mild-mannered ranger friend peering through the bars at the state penitentiary, hence I told the truth: we hadn't actually seen anyone flipping the rocks. It was a close call. Hoover had scared me silly.

I decided to "get" Puskar if it were the last thing I'd ever do. I didn't have a plan, but figured I'd enlist the services of the Dangerous Dillman, and we'd play it by ear. The following June, on a hot afternoon, the three of us headed down Pine Creek to check a favorite den. About a mile from the vehicle, after making a tough ascent, we were nearing the spot. From the opposite direction, what sounded like and appeared to be a violent thunderstorm was approaching. Dillman could read my mind— we'd keep hunting until the last possible second, then beat a hasty retreat to the truck. Puskar, wearing his slippery-soled, bargain-bin boots, would probably fall and be overrun by the storm; if the lightning didn't get him, hypothermia would. Upon arriving at the den, Al, seemingly engrossed in trying to establish a telepathic link with a yellow rattler, lost touch with the signs of fury in the looming thunderheads. When the moment was right, we made the dash. A quarter-mile into the run, Al was falling farther and farther behind; when we couldn't see him anymore, we increased our pace.

Vicious winds, sheets of rain, and slamming thunderbolts were on our heels as Gary and I reached the truck. Fifteen minutes passed before the storm subsided. We speculated regarding which ambulance service would be sent in to retrieve Puskar. We decided to phone Al's wife to ask if she wanted us to notify a rescue squad.

When I fired up the Powerwagon to head for town, Al stepped out of the brush. He said he continued to run, even after being overtaken by the turbulent storm. Losing his footing on the narrow, greasy path, he slipped, sliding twenty feet downslope and into the run at the bottom of the ravine; it took several minutes for him to find his glasses and claw his way back to the trail. When I saw Al again, several months later, he had neatly repaired his specs with white medic's tape.

I upheld my vow to stymie Puskar; however, it took some time. One morning, Al and I were heading down 414 at a pretty good clip, discussing which ridge we'd hunt first. As we rounded a sharp curve, a flock of small yellowish birds scrambled from the center of the roadway. One of them didn't make it. Al, being a member and past president of the local Audubon chapter, ordered me to stop and back up. I got the impression that he was going to attempt to breathe life back into the pile of guts and feathers or give the thing a ceremonial burial of sorts. He got out and rushed to the remains, gently scooping them into his hands for further scrutiny. I rolled down my window. "Sparrow?" I scoffed. Al mumbled something. "What?" I barked.

"Pine siskin," he softly replied. "You killed a pine siskin." I felt sorry for the bird. I don't like to needlessly or accidentally kill any creature, but Puskar's reaction to the situation triggered me into a severe laughing fit. At that moment, Puskar disowned me. The man is dangerous—multiply by two.

I met Jimm Leach when we became classmates at the community college. He invited me along to his hometown area of Galeton one fall weekend to hunt turkeys. I didn't have much experience in that field, but he assured me that, with his turkey wisdom and prior experience, we'd probably score within an hour or so following the crack of dawn. We'd leave Friday evening and, taking sleeping bags, spend the night on the mountain he intended to hunt. The weather report sounded decent, so we headed north.

As we arrived at the eastern end of Galeton, a blizzard was entering the western end. We hung out in the local restaurant until they closed up. Around midnight we made the climb on T.V. Tower Mountain in Leach's Beetle. (It would have made a grand commercial for Volkswagen, but the vehicle was a bit short-changed on the sleeping accommodations end.) The temperature was ten outside and four below in the Beetle. Quickly computing the wind chill with Jimm's pocket survival booklet, we decided to try sleeping in the car. By daybreak, we were exhausted, shivering, and a bit hungry. When the hour of hunting was up, we headed back to the restaurant. I congratulated him for making a gallant effort and asked him to take me home.

One Saturday in July, Leach, a few other guys, and I met at an organized rattlesnake roundup held on a private, enclosed, hunting preserve. We had no intention of helping rid the "pay to hunt" enclosure of snakes, but we were always interested in snooping through some new territory. Jimm, toting a portfolio of maps and aerial photos of the place, determined we'd have to jump the fence, leaving the snake hunt's official boundary, if we were to see any rattlers. He led us and several other innocents to the far corner of the impoundment. Beyond the fence we could see a wall of yellow, white, and orange "no trespass" posters stapled in tiers to *every* boundary tree. Leach assured us that "most" of the owners of large, forested tracts, like the one we were staring at, didn't mind trespassers who were hunting rattlers. "Anyway," he said, "these guys probably don't come around 'til deer season."

The seven of us scaled the ten-foot fence, leaving the preserve behind. As we stood on an old logging road looking over Jimm's maps and deciding what to do, a truck entered the scene. We scattered like a flock of turkeys that had accidentally walked in front of a bobcat den. We couldn't get back together. Every time one of the boys would holler, the others would run deeper into the laurel, and Leach was the only one with a map.

After several hours of hiding, I found my way back to the fence and reentered the enclosure. Trying to get back to headquarters was nearly impossible as huge, horned exotic beasts, some weighing in at a ton, kept blocking my route. I was also a little nervous about running into an overheated wild boar, knowing that, with a favorable wind, my snub-nosed .38 loaded with wadcutters has the knock-down power of a small ball-peen hammer. After a bit of pussyfooting, I made it back to our vehicle to find Leach sipping on a cool beverage. He asked me what had taken so long. I explained about not wanting to pay a $300 trespassing fine and the gauntlet of wooly goliaths. He told me they were American bison. I told him to give me a break—the natives wouldn't have made it through the first winter had they depended on killing the animals I saw with arrows. Leach is extremely dangerous.

Michael Machmer, known as "Woodsy" by some and "the Midget" by others, accompanied me on a Bodine Mountain excursion one evening; it was his first rattlesnake hunt. Embarking from Route 14 at the steepest incline I could find, I planned to break him in properly. Halfway up the grade I was praying for my second wind to kick in, while the Midget was still chomping at the bit; the only reason he waited for me was that he wasn't exactly sure what we were looking for. Since it was early in the season and late in the day (the air was a bit chilly), by the time we reached the denning area, the snakes were down under; thus I was severely ridiculed. (This wasn't the first time I'd been chastised as an inferior guide, but I hadn't begun to recover from the emotional damage of being outwinded by a greenhorn.)

When we started back down to the highway, I duped the Midget into a downhill race, knowing he was feeling smug and probably forgetting about his trick knee. Several rods into the duel I noticed that Mike was leveling into a dead run, his legs churning like eggbeaters and his body perpendicular to the steep grade. Having to maintain a respectable showing, for fear he'd let up before his knee dislocated, I abandoned all caution. Within a blink of making such a foolhardy decision, I was unwillingly performing a cartwheel-like maneuver that would have stunned the judges at an international gymnastics

competition. As I regained consciousness, I guessed that I was in Never-Never Land; but when the pigwidgeon standing over me crowed, "What's the matter, couldn't ya keep up?", I knew I was still on Bodine Mountain. The Midget found the lens that had popped from my eyeglasses, offering to return with his metal detector to search for the temple.

Even though I was nearing full consciousness when we reached the vehicle, I handed Mike the keys; I couldn't drive safely without my glasses. I flagged him on, to no avail, as we approached the Forest Inn; he assured me that "a little" brew would speed the healing process. Yes, it pays to have friends like the Midget to help you when you're down. The remedy worked—within three weeks I felt almost normal. Someday, I truly hope to fully repay my good pal, the Midget.

It took me quite a while to discover that my neighbor, Roger Learn, is a displaced flatlander—he can mimic a ridgerunner better than any flatlander I know. He asked me if he could trail along on a snake hunt some day and make a video to show his biology students. I thought it was a great idea, saying, "Let's go!" Roger said we'd have to wait until he made a trip to New Jersey

to pick up his parents' camera. I inquired as to why his folks were in New Jersey; he told me that when they retired, they headed for the shore for health reasons.

Early on a fresh June morning we headed for the hills, settling details of our plan of attack during the drive. We wanted the program to appear as professional as possible. Roger had little experience with a camcorder and I had none. We had no knowledge of editing or whatever doctoring is necessary to make a good video from a tape full of miscellaneous garbage, therefore we had prepared a detailed script and were determined not to deviate or make taping errors. Near Liberty, as Roger fondled the camera and recited cameraman tactics, a herd of deer bounded across the highway. Our tape now has a shaky opening scene, shot through the windshield of my Bronco, of brown and white spots flipping through goldenrod. Farther down the highway, I pointed out a bluebird sitting on a fencepost; consequently, the second scene of our "professional" timber rattlesnake "film" is what appears to be a blue dot on top of a stick.

When we arrived at our destination, we got out the script. I made an introductory speech, then shot a scene of Roger crossing the stream on a fallen tree; he taped me climbing the steep mountainside through the blossoming laurel. As we climbed, I told him I'd give another short talk at the top of the hill. When we reached the crest, I turned around and said, "Give me a cue when you want me to start"; he already had the tape rolling. Soon afterward, I spotted some basking rattlers and called for Roger. It was his first encounter with the snakes in the wild. He trained the camera on a snake and began filming. I picked up the snake with my stick and set it on a rock closer to Roger; he began backpedaling and swinging the camera spastically, trying to put the critter back in the viewfinder. After things calmed down, he became awestruck at the sight of a large yellow phase, which was fully stretched and basking in the morning sun. He sat down on a nearby log and began taping—it was the longest motionless stint Roger ever performed, I suspect. The tape now has a fifteen-minute segment of a sleeping snake in which the sounds of a woodpecker and an airplane are the highlights.

The next scene was to be on another ridge. After hiking for twenty minutes through head-high laurel, I started another speech; the camera battery fizzled.

The following Saturday, we were on the road again with a higher-priced battery pack. We wore the same clothes as before, trying to fabricate the illusion of a one-day adventure. Taping went pretty smoothly at the first den site, including another fifteen-minute dose of motionless snake. When we reached the second den, I spotted the flank of what I thought to be, judging from scale size, a pretty good snake. I hollered, "Here's a big one!" Roger raced over, trained the camera on me, and very deliberately announced, "Curt has just located a really big snake." Seconds later, I extracted the snake, which was not nearly as large as I'd estimated. Camera rolling, with an obviously disappointed change of tune, Roger asked, "Is *that* the big one?"

The final segment, according to our script, required a laborious climb in the afternoon heat. On the rim of the mountain, I stood on a ledge and spewed a boring dissertation on safety in rattlesnake country. Roger was off to the side so he could frame me and a yellow rattler that was one step below me on the ledge. I could see that Roger was getting tired of my lecture. Sweat was streaming down his face. I could hear him snorting violently as he tried to discharge a gnat from his nostril. Terminating the speech, I moved around the ledge in order to capture the snake. I murmured, "There are two of 'em." Roger thought I said, "I can't find 'im."

He exclaimed, "Right there!" I thought he was indicating the presence of yet another snake.

I replied, "What?"

Then he cracked. With a distinct coastal plain accent, he screeched, "It's right there in front of your face!"

Upon returning home, Roger and I viewed the tape. We, of course, were quite tickled with our first wildlife documentary. Roger, overwhelmed by his new role as a producer and his close encounters with timber rattlesnakes, totally forgot about the educational purposes of our undertaking. He sped away to a local sporting goods dealer who he said had connections with the outdoor video industry.

9

First and Last Time

EW NATURE LOVERS REALIZE THAT MAGNETIC compasses are virtually useless on the laurel-infested flat-tops of Northcentral Pennsylvania. As proof, I refer to the Second Annual Hunt for Tome's Cave, conducted on the third weekend of March 1991.

In his book, *Pioneer Life; or, Thirty Years a Hunter,* Philip Tome gives rough directions to, and describes, a cave that his party discovered while hunting elk near Cedar Run in 1811. In his detailed and enchanting description he refers to it as having an "artificial appearance" and as being "quite a curiosity." The area has its share of rocks and ledges, but is not considered cave country. Some readers think the story is a gross exaggeration, at best; but they'll *never* prove it. Only us believers have the opportunity to prove something.

Sixteen of us lined up, spaced at hundred-foot intervals, along a road in the Algerines. Every third man had a compass, being instructed to hold course during the half-mile-long grid search. Shortly into the drive, dense laurel encroached on both flanks. A quarter-mile from the starting point we all funneled into a small ravine where we argued for some time over proper compass use. No one realized that the laurel caused the devices to go bonkers. Later that day, just the opposite occurred; this time, the middle of the line encountered the point of a wedge-shaped patch of laurel. The compasses went haywire again causing us to break into two groups for the remainder of the day.

Knowing for years of the uselessness of compasses in laurel, I left mine home the afternoon I took the neighbor boy, Adam Rutty, on a rattlesnake hunt. We drove along the Bodine Mountain Road, which hadn't seen a road grader for over a decade. It took some finagling to snake a route around the multitude of boulders that were sticking out of the road far enough to poke halfway through an engine block. When we reached the dead end we hiked across the flat for a mile. I had no problem going by the sun on that crystal clear afternoon; hence, we directly found the den.

Fascinated by a section of ledges I'd missed during my first hunt in the area, I failed to notice a swiftly approaching storm front that blocked the western sky, shortening the evening considerably. By the time we decided to head out, there was no visible clue to the setting sun's position. I assured Adam there was no problem since I knew of an old, dim trail that would take us to a main logging road that led to the truck. After thirty minutes of hiking across the flat and seeing the same spot on an unfamiliar boundary line for the third time, I told Adam that we didn't have enough daylight remaining to make the truck even if I knew where it was. "It's gonna be pitch dark in fifteen minutes," he reminded me.

An intense wall of electrical disturbances flashing between the earth and the atmosphere appeared to be systematically annihilating everything in its path as it marched toward us. Since it wasn't the first time I'd been slightly disoriented, I was only semipanicky; I was concerned that Adam's folks might never speak to me again if, for some reason, we didn't survive the ordeal. Detecting the shoulder of the ridge, we jumped ship, heading down a steep side during the last few minutes of visibility. I had no idea which direction the drainage was leading us—the possibilities were frightening according to my foggy recollection of the map I'd left at home with the compass.

A short while later, guided by flashes of still distant lightning, we were resting comfortably in a cozy hunting cabin in Grays Run. The time-honored gentleman who kindly received us offered to haul us back to our vehicle, which was eight miles distant via dirt roads. As we crested Bodine Mountain, the full fury of the storm was swirling on the ridge top; sharp gusts bowed the timber while lightning danced about highlighting the action. "This is a bad mountain to be on during a storm," the gent said as he lowered the accelerator on his new Isuzu Trooper. "I left my power saw at camp. We gotta get off the mountain before a tree blocks the road behind us," he added. I didn't realize a four-by-four could stand such punishment, outside of Hollywood, but the seasoned mountaineer knew better as he careened across the rocks I'd carefully avoided earlier in the day. I braced myself, expecting the undercarriage to be cleanly sheared from the vehicle at any second.

At the end of the road, two lightning strikes in rapid succession within a stone's throw of my truck made us think twice about getting out. Adam and I made the dash, and by 11:00 P.M. we were home. When the concerned women asked why we hadn't called, I simply said that the Bodine Mountain phone booth had been vandalized.

The next time I asked Adam if he'd like to go snake hunting with me, he said he hadn't procured a space blanket or flare gun and thought he'd better pass—typical of the one-shot partners I always wind up with.

Even my own brother-in-law, Jeff, refuses to accompany me on local "wilderness experiences" following our snake hunt a few years ago. He stopped at the house one evening, en route home from a business trip in Syracuse. Learning that he'd be in the area again in a few weeks, I asked him if he'd like to go on a hunt. As we discussed the details, I started to suggest that he knock off a few pounds prior to the hunt, which sent him running to his car to fetch the remaining half of a large pizza with everything on it that he'd been munching on earlier in the evening. The next morning I made Jeff a large bowl of nutritious oatmeal, topped with skim milk and a quarter teaspoon of maple syrup. Sending him off with a container of the same for lunch, I instructed him to stick to the daily diet until I saw him again. He phoned later in the week to tell me the plan was working. He said that each day he'd spread oatmeal on half the pizza—and that's the half he wouldn't eat.

The day of our scheduled hike was a real scorcher, preceded by a month's drought. We climbed a long slope near Slate Run during the so-called cool of the morning, nearly collapsing from heat exhaustion upon reaching the summit. Naturally, I'd talked Jeff into leaving his canteen in the car, promising him a royal celebration at the local watering hole if he proved worthy. About a mile farther back on the ridge, I began frantically searching for a spring seep. We finally found a feeble spring hole that was a whisker away from being stagnant; I slurped first, giving Jeff confidence to follow suit, and assured him that a little bacteria was far less deadly than heat stroke, at least for a while.

After floundering through mountaintop rocks and laurel for several hours, seeing only a few dwarf rattlers, I suggested we leave the despicable wasteland; Jeff, who hadn't spoken for some time, nodded his approval. When we reached the stream at the foot of the mountain I crawled out on a slab rock in order to peer at a school of trout tucked alongside. When I looked up, I saw Jeff crossing the creek about fifty yards downstream. I hooted, flagging him up to see the fish; he hesitated, staring at me for a short while, then slowly plodded over. (Had I been a properly trained and equipped paramedic, at that point I would have been radioing for Life Flight.) He looked at the fish, then silently returned to the crossing. The climb out of the ravine was the "one step up, slip back two" type. I hoed my way up to the forestry road where I sat in semidelirium on the berm. A few minutes later, a passing forest ranger stopped to offer me a lift. At the sound of the idling truck, Jeff, who'd been lying a little way down the slope, crawled up to the road. Cooled by the airy ride in the pickup, I regained my faculties enough to needle Jeff about being an overweight flatlander who shouldn't be allowed in the woods.

A week later, after six days of diarrhea and fever, I phoned Jeff to see if he was in a similar state. Elaine, my sister-in-law, informed me that he was doing fine except for the silver-dollar-sized blisters on his feet. I told her I was fine also, then hung up and dialed the clinic to arrange for a giardiasis test.

Johnny Engel, another of my brothers-in-law, probably should have learned his lesson the first time I took him rattle-snake hunting—but, of course, he was only eight years old. I can still hear him squealing—I held him out over the Band Rock Ledge, trying to get him used to heights. But Johnny is tough, and he hung in there for twenty more years of abuse—until last summer. My father-in-law, Howdy, called me one evening in mid-August. He said that he and Johnny had undertaken a project to clean up an old dump site on a ridge in northern Lycoming County. When they walked around it to size things up, they saw a "lunker" of a yellow rattler. He said it was bigger than any he'd ever seen. I wasn't in snake mode at the time and had been on enough wild-goose snake chases to know that the chance of finding that snake the next day was slim. I told him I'd probably check the place out . . . sometime.

Late the next afternoon, Johnny phoned: "You're gonna have to get down here! I took the loader into the side of the dump, and there were rattlers all over the place! And we saw the yella one, and ya ain't gonna get 'im with that little hook on the end of your stick!" I told him I'd meet him on the mountain in forty-five minutes, hit the phone's clicker, and dialed for reinforcements. Fifteen minutes later my wife, Donna, Mike Machmer, and I were halfway to Roaring Branch and gaining altitude. I didn't want to waste time—Johnny is a borderline ecologist. I knew he'd done his part by telling me about the situation; if I didn't start separating the rattlers from the appliances and sofas, the serpents would be wearing a water heater in a day or so. He wasn't about to work around the rattlers, nor would he neatly package them for delivery to an animal shelter. Planning the strategy in favor of the snakes as we drove, I asked his big sister: "Donna, what are we gonna do with the snakes?"

"Keep 'em 'til they clean the place up, then take 'em back," she answered.

"Yeah, but how long is it gonna take 'em? If I don't turn 'em loose in two weeks, they might not make it back to their den."

"I'll tell Johnny to get his butt in gear," Donna replied.

The sun was bearing down on the distant ridgeline by the time we arrived at the dump site; there was a damp chill in the air. Howdy, John, and his wife, Michelle, climbed out of their truck, which was parked just shy of the trash heap. "Pretty cool," Mike noted.

"They might be down," I agreed, as we forwarded our gear to the edge of the debris pile. Donna removed the lid from our fifteen-gallon plastic snake drum. Dad and John led us over to the side where their crawler-loader sat. John pointed, "Check there, next to those tires." Dad added, "The big yellow one's been hangin' out next to that water heater."

Mike and I tiptoed across the nail-riddled boards, washing machines, and bedsprings, trying to sneak in without falling headlong into the musty, twisted maze. We'd momentarily stopped several feet shy of the tire pile to scrutinize the suspect snake hotel when I noticed a pair of beady, black eyes staring at me from beneath a four-foot-square chunk of gray foam rubber. I motioned to Mike saying, "Pull the corner back." As I lifted the exposed rattler out of its nest, I noticed another one tucked farther back in. I hollered, "There's more!" while hurrying toward our holding container. Dad was coming across the trash with the drum, but I motioned him back—I knew that if the snake made a run off my stick when I tried to feed it into the plastic drum, it would slip down into rat heaven in a blink. After

I pulled the second snake out, Mike yanked the foam back and captured the third.

We moved back in and started carefully pawing through the half-dozen tires that lay near the water heater—nothing. Mike raised the water heater, hoping we'd find the big one; but Big Yeller had given us the slip when we were sneaking in the first time, no doubt. While we scoured the rest of the main junk pile, Dad and John started flipping boards and sofas along the perimeter. They kicked an eight-foot-long chunk of loosely rolled carpet that was lying near the bucket of the crawler. When we joined them on the perimeter search, Mike hooked the same roll of carpet and spun it around, trying to draw a buzz. I raised the end and glanced down through to make sure it was empty, then dropped it; as I walked on, I looked back in time to see a forty-six-inch black phase scoot from the far end and into the crawler bucket! Donna chuckled; Michelle shrieked, "You guys checked that thing four times!"

With the evening's hunt winding down, we congregated at Johnny's pickup for a tailgate chat. I asked John to hold off on the cleanup operation for a few days, to give me a chance to remove more rattlers; he agreed. Donna asked him how long the job would take. He indicated that since Dad and he could only work at it part-time, it might be a while. Donna said, "Curt'll have to let 'em go pretty soon or they'll freeze trying to get back to their den."

"Where's the den?" he asked.

"I don't know," I answered. "They could've come from different ones, maybe a mile away." John hunkered down, spit a stream of tobacco juice into the laurel, and began scratching and jabbing the sandy road surface with a short stick. Dad's face broke into a grin, and he turned, wandering toward the crawler to check the oil. John began politely explaining the disastrous consequences in store if he were to discover that I'd released the snakes within two or three miles of the job site before Dad and he had completed the cleanup. I said that I knew of a biologist who was studying rattlesnake translocation. "He'll take 'em," I said.

During the following week, I made several more trips to the dump, capturing two more snakes. I called Clark Shiffer, of the Fish Commission, to let him know that I was over the limit for capturing snakes and to discuss their fate. He said, "I don't know, Howie might take 'em." I called Howard Reinert, who was already in the midst of his translocation study; he had no need for more snakes. He told me that if I didn't release the rattlers in close proximity to the capture site, they'd probably be doomed; I knew that if I did, and Johnny recognized any of them, the snakes and I would both be doomed—a double doom it would be. But I knew what I was going to do: double-cross Johnny—and, since I was doing the work of the Lord, it would be acceptable.

I stayed tuned to the progress of the cleanup project through Donna's phone conversations with family members, but I was getting pretty itchy after two weeks. The snakes had been well fed at their old retreat, evidenced by the number of times I had to clean their two holding pens; however, fresh water and a romp in the lawn once in a while wasn't pacifying them or me—it was time to take them home.

On the last Sunday in August, I heard that the boys were about finished—just had to smooth things up a bit. On Monday evening, my eleven-year-old son, Adam, and I loaded the plastic drums into the Bronco and headed south. On our way up the mountain road, I kept my fingers crossed, hoping that Johnny and Dad had seen enough of the place over the weekend. "What are we gonna tell Uncle Johnny if he asks us where we put the snakes?" Adam quizzed.

"See that rockslide over there? That's where we put 'em— OK?"

"But isn't that like lyin'?"

"Not really, see. It's all right to lie like heck, so long as it's

God's will, see—like in this case—we're savin' his precious creatures."

"Yeah, but in Adam and Eve, the snakes aren't any good."

"I know all that; but rattlesnakes wasn't around then—he invented them later. Anyway, it's late in the season; these snakes are gonna head for their den before Johnny comes back up here—it's gettin' cold."

On the mountaintop, we discovered only the crawler and a patch of bare ground where the heap of trash had stood for years. We gently tipped the containers, allowing the rattlers to ease out on their own. We leaned back against the Bronco, watching three of them slither into the laurel on our right; the other three headed opposite. For five minutes we listened intently as they slowly crawled across the crispy-dry leaves. Then the largest male, the forty-six-incher, returned to the release point, smelled around for a minute, and left again. Adam and I remained, listening to a louder rustling from the head-high laurel down the road. Soon, a bear broke out of the laurel and onto the road. "What are we gonna do?" Adam hissed as the small bruin ambled toward us.

"See how close he gets," I whispered. I wanted to see what it would do when it caught a whiff of rattlesnake. But it continued ambling indifferently past the containers and to within eight feet of us, whereupon I cut loose a frantic war whoop, which sent it crashing through the brush. Adam said, "What did ya do that for?"

Two weeks passed, during which I prayed that the rattlers had beat a safe retreat toward their dens, for their sakes and mine. It was Sunday afternoon and my family and I were going to a birthday party in Williamsport—and Uncle Johnny would be there. It was a fair day. Following the ceremonies, the men were milling around outdoors, having a chew and chewing the fat. It wasn't long until Johnny's towering hulk was hovering over me, "Ya know, Dad and I went back up last Saturday to smooth things up."

"How'd ya make out?" I asked.

"When I climbed on the machine, a big black rattler went shootin' off the track on the other side; and I jumped down."

"No kiddin', that makes eight of 'em includin' the big yella one we didn't get," I quickly replied.

He continued, "Then we spotted another one layin' right in the middle o' where the dump used to be." At that point, my right eyelid began to flutter uncontrollably; but thanks to my photosensitive, tinted eyeglasses, John didn't notice. "Then Dad found another one down the road about a hundred feet."

"Holy smokes! That place was crawlin' with rattlers—six we caught, plus Big Yeller, then them three! Geez! Hey, I'm gonna grab another hunk o' cake 'fore it's all gone!"

I never asked Johnny what he did with the three snakes, and he never asked me what I did with the six; but I can just imagine—and so can he.

10

Secret Spots

HE NATURAL FEATURES OF NORTHCENTRAL PENN-
sylvania attract droves of local and nonresident visitors
every year, especially the outdoorsy and history-buff types.
High Knob, Colton Point, or Bucktail Drive might do the trick
for those who prefer motor tours. A short walk will land others
at Bark Cabin, Barbour Rock, or Rock Run. The able-bodied,
more adventurous individuals often head for Fahnestock Ridge,
the Black Forest Trail, or Four-Mile Falls. The daredevil types
are periodically seen climbing the Blue Run Rocks, crawling
through the McIntyre Mines, and gliding from Hyner View. For
Northcentral hunters, all these places are great for family out-
ings and off-season pacifiers; however, finding the ultimate
"secret spot" is what everyone hopes for—the buck hotel, the
bear crossing, the trout hideaway, the gobbler roost.

Regularly accused by affluent egotists (who cannot—or will
not—understand the lure of raw nature) of being simple-
minded, I reap great satisfaction in discovering my very own
unique pieces of turf—my secret spots. Whenever I appear to be
fishing a new stream, hunting turkeys on a new ridge, or looking
for a rattler on a new hillside, I'm actually waiting for a secret
spot. I say "waiting" because I never find secret spots when I'm
searching for them. When I least suspect it, they spring forth
and throttle me; they overwhelm me; there's no way of mistak-
ing them for a normal place. They are always void of litter,
human tracks, and sounds of civilization; a trail within close
proximity of a secret spot is unheard of. The air is always crisp—

free of pesky insects; a smooth, fallen pine snag is normally on hand to provide comfortable seating while I'm being mesmerized by a shimmering brookie, gobbling bronze beauty, or singing velvet tail.

The first encounter with a secret spot is the best. The sooner you return to the spot, the sooner it loses its mystique. It becomes worn-out; it becomes just any-old-place. As a matter of fact, I recommend you never return to a secret spot. If you do, it may not appear the least bit unique even on the second rendezvous, resulting in disappointment. I mentioned earlier that secret spots manifest themselves suddenly, originating out of nowhere. That "nowhere" is a medley of weather conditions, season, time of day, aromas, participating flora and fauna, and your own state of mind. The timer, the magnet, the host—the Mastermind—remains the "secret" in secret spots. Cherish the memory and don't return. The mystique will escalate; you'll have a burning desire to return. Put it off as long as possible. It's always refreshing to have something to look forward to. If you wait long enough, on your second visit, if you're lucky, you won't find the place. Chances are you'll walk right to the spot and not recognize it. You'll return home wondering if that was the place, or if you missed it, or if you saw it in your dreams. Then, go back into the woods, somewhere new, and wait for another secret spot.

I still have a few good secret spots tucked away—Standing Stone Den, Indian Millstone, and Buzzard Cave. These favorite secret spots are in the upper ledges—that's why they're good ones. Slobs that tote soft drinks into the forest usually gulp them down and heave the aluminum long before they reach the upper ledges; and all-terrain vehicles don't leave tracks on cliffs.

My best secret spot is Mystery Rocks. I discovered them in the early 1970s while I was mapping forest pest activity from a small aircraft. I carefully circled the spot on my map, marking the location of the twin boulder fields I saw. For years I anticipated seeing those rocks from ground level, knowing they'd be teem-

ing with northern rattlesnakes. I kept the map tucked in my
secret spot file for a day when I'd need a good fix. Last season,
my outdoor enthusiasm hitting rock bottom, I invited several
old snake-hunting cronies to join me for a hunt at Rattlesnake
Hunter's Heaven (former name of Mystery Rocks). It would be a
reunion during which, I professed, I would prove to be the
greatest timber rattler hunter of all time. I smirked at the boys'
snide Doubting Thomas remarks that started just two hours into
our hike. Several hours later, after crisscrossing the ridge four
times in the area where I'd plotted the rocks, my old friends
became downright mutinous. I was finally forced to call off the
search, promising I'd find the mother of all dens under better
circumstances—by myself.

After I find Mystery Rocks, I'll take on Tome's Cave, then the
Lost Silver Mine. Secret spots are great!

11

"Blood Full of Venom"

ON A FRESH, SUNNY MORNING—ANY FRESH, sunny morning—in late May or June, there are some fellows in the Northern Tier that are stricken by a tenacious desire to head for the ridges. They are driven to hike, to climb, to struggle through neck-high laurel—to find timber rattlers. Prior to snake hunting regulations, some of them hunted for bounty, market, and organized hunt entries. Now, many continue to hunt for competition "trophy" snakes or for "special request" specimens; but the majority of their hunting is "catch and release."

I contacted six of these diehard rattler hunters in July 1992, and to my surprise they all agreed to be interviewed. Some of their friends and neighbors call these men "crazy," "possessed," "foolish," or "stupid." Could be, for they probably wouldn't stop hunting rattlers to save their lives.

Between 1978 and 1987, Mike Rachiele of Gaines collected eight trophies for the longest timber rattler entered at organized snake hunts—four at Morris, two at Cross Fork, and two at Sinnemahoning.

"I promised Patsy [Mike's wife] I'd quit hunting when I won a trophy at Morris, but—well—I won in '83, '84, '86, and '87.

"I started hunting eighteen or twenty years ago on the day of the Cross Fork Hunt. Jimm Leach and Rawley Grant invited me to go along. We went down on the Fahnestock. I found a small rattler, maybe a twenty-seven-incher. I had one of those turtle hooks, you know, and I just kind of stood there staring at the snake. Jimm and Rawley were on out the ridge. Finally I said to myself, 'You're gonna have to reach down and get it on the hook if you're gonna put it in the bag.' I got it in my blood. I just took off.

"I sold a lot of rattlers. I hate to admit it—but, yeah, mostly to individuals down at Cross Fork's hunt. We had a big sign 'Snakes for Sale'; we'd get from ten to twenty dollars apiece. If I would have taken a hundred snakes, I would have sold 'em all. People—guys up to camp—wanted 'em to take home so they could say, 'Look what I caught,' you know.

"I got a dry bite, just once; the fangs just kind of scratched me. I shouldn't have been fooling with 'em, the condition I was in at the time; but, you know, it was on a bet. I learned my lesson. I said, 'That's it. No more stunts.' My partner spent the night in the hospital once. He flung a bag full of snakes over his back. I kept telling him, 'You're gonna get bit,' and he kept saying, 'Nope.' All the sudden, he dropped the bag; it kind of went rolling down the hill. He said, 'I've been bit!' By the time I fetched the bag of snakes back up the hill, he had his shirt off and was hollerin', 'Where is it! Where is it!' To me, it looked like a bee sting. I looked the bag over and found a fang sticking out. I took him to the hospital. He was all right. Yeah, he had a lot of snakes in that bag; you could see that one fang sticking through the side.

"I know of one snake that would have went over sixty inches, easily, the way they measure them at the hunts. It was after the hunts, so I left it go. If I would have kept it, it would have wound up mounted. I didn't want to see that. I saw it once since then. I wanted to catch him for a hunt. He got back under a rock and I had to let go of 'im. I don't believe in hurting them; I'd rather have 'em get away. I learned years ago, you just don't flip those rocks. It ruins the dens.

"I never hunted for the bounty, but my neighbor used to, years ago. He'd kill close to three hundred a year sometimes. I never liked to see the snakes killed. They were all individuals—

you could tell 'em apart. I'd wind up leaving most of 'em go. I could get a rattler out of a cageful and remember which den it came from. I'd put 'em back where they belonged. Sometimes I'd have to transplant them, even though, you know, it doesn't work most of the time. If I would hear of a place where people were going into a den and killing the snakes, I'd hunt it through and pick up the survivors. Word would get around and they'd lay off. If I didn't, they'd keep going back until they'd shot 'em all.

"The rattler population is nowhere near what it was even five years ago. They're on the decline. I just like to take pictures of them anymore—I might pick up a big one for a contest, then let it go. The last really good den I knew of had about thirty snakes. I took only three big ones out during a two-year period. Then some fellow on a dirt bike discovered the place. He was telling about it down at the store. Someone overheard him tellin' and went right up to the den and took 'em all. Sold most of 'em I guess. You can go up there now and see three snakes, if it's a good day and you're lucky. I knew of about thirty pretty good dens, ten or fifteen years ago. Now, I know of about a dozen places, maybe, where I could take someone to see snakes, but we'd be lucky to find one to three at each den.

"It's good that they're putting some restrictions on the hunting. The Fish Commission is trying to help. It won't be long, I think, that they'll have the snake on the Endangered Species list. The best thing they did was ban the sale of 'em. They should probably do some work around the dens, but most of the guys wouldn't want to show them where their favorite dens are. I know of a few dens where, just in the last ten years, between the overgrowth and the turkey buzzards moving in, you don't see any snakes anymore."

Well-known at the Morris Snake Hunt is Gary Wier of the Brookside area. Hunting since 1962, Gary has captured rattlers throughout Lycoming and Tioga counties, primarily for the hunt, where he some-

*times serves on the pit crew. Occasionally, he hunts with partners with
names like Linda, Michele, Kelly, and Kristy.*

"I'd hunt out Cold Run, and then across the main crick, then
down and circle back. I carried a pedometer once; it was twelve
miles. I'd carry extra bags. Whatever I caught in Cold Run I'd
drop 'em off; then I'd pick 'em up on the way back through. I
hunted that route one day—it was sort of a bad day—and I only
picked up a couple in Cold Run. So I hunted across and on
down and—nothin'. I started down toward an old log road
down in the bottom—headin' home, you know, a little bit dis-
gusted—when I saw a spot up on the sidehill that looked pretty
good. If I saw a spot that looked good, I'd have to check it out; I
couldn't walk by it. So I walked up. It was built up sort of high
with sandstones. I climbed up on and looked over the edge.
There was probably twenty-five to thirty rattlers layin' there. I
only caught a dozen of 'em; the rest of 'em got down under.
That was the most I ever saw at once.

"If ya hunted with somebody, it wasn't so bad, you know; ya
had somebody to hold the bag. Course, I've hunted with several
people that didn't like holdin' the bag. Course, I didn't like
holdin' the bag for some people either. I guided a big crew once
in a while—friends, relatives, and some guys from a professional
hockey team; we'd have about twenty people. I'd try to get 'em to
spread out, figurin' we could cover a lot of ground. But it never
worked out very well; there was times when, if I walked around
a tree three times, everybody walked around the same tree three
times—it was 'follow the snake hunter.' . . .

"There's a few places that used to be good, but the timber's
grown up. Where the stone was all white and exposed—good
habitat—now it's moss covered and—no snakes. The rattler
population is down quite a lot, at least in this area. They're down
80 percent from what they used to be. Guess I'm responsible for
a lot of that. I think they'll make it though. I don't know; you still
have people that, you know, if they see one, they have to kill it—
no matter where it's at. I can understand people that don't want

'em around their house. But if ya go a couple miles back in the woods and see a snake, I don't think ya ought to just kill it cause it's a 'terrible snake.' But a lot of people do.

"I had about twenty or more spots where I could pretty much depend on gettin' snakes. There's some left; but there's some that I cleaned out. This older fella from a camp told me about his nephew bein' up on this big stone in archery season the year before. He got to lookin' around, and he was surrounded by rattlers. He went about half nuts, firin' all his broadheads at these snakes. He killed a few of 'em. So the old gent took me up there, and I caught nine. I went there many, many times and got 'em; I probably took a hundred snakes out of there. When some of these guys were in camp, they'd go up there with shotguns and kill any they saw. The last couple of times I've been there, it's been just spider webs over the holes—no snakes.

"My wife, Linda, and I and another couple were out huntin' one evening, down toward Larrys Crick. We had five or six snakes in the bag in the trunk of the car when we were done. We stopped at a bar up on Oregon Hill, then went down to Little Pine Tavern. It got late, and they gave us last call. Then they gave us one more. It was probly three in the morning when we asked them for another drink. They said, 'No, we gotta close; you guys gotta go home.' So I said, 'I got a bag of snakes out in the car. If you don't give us a drink, I'm gonna bring 'em in here and dump 'em.' The owner's friend was tendin' bar; he was from the city, and he was scared of snakes. So he gave us a drink. Then we asked for another one. He said, 'Nope. Do what ya want, you ain't gettin' no more drinks.' So I went out and opened the trunk of the car, and I took the bag and shook it—got 'em to rattlin'. So he says, 'OK, OK, you can have another drink.' So I put the snakes back in the car, and we got another drink. So, it was gettin' along to be about five in the morning and I asked for another drink. He said, 'Nope.' I said, 'I'm gonna bring those snakes back in.' He said, 'Well do what ya gotta.' So I brought 'em in and dumped 'em right out on the floor. He jumped right over the bar, run to the men's room, and stood on the toilet. He yells, 'You can have anything you want!' My buddy and I went behind the bar and started settin' everybody up; Linda went out and got the catcher and started gatherin' the snakes up.

"Yeah, Linda used to hunt with me quite a bit. We were down here, one day, on a steep side. I'd gone down over—there was a big flat stone I wanted to check—and it was so steep I had to hold on to a saplin' down there; and there was four or five snakes. She's got the bag, so I hollered at her to come down and help me. So she's up there walkin' along this ledge; and she starts workin' the grabbers into the brush like crazy. Pretty soon she just throwed them grabbers and reached down and yanked this four-footer out of the brush by its tail. Yeah, she got chewed out over that one. Our girls, Michele, Kelly, and Kristy used to go, too. Michele used to take the grabber and the bag, and jump on her horse, and head for the mountain."

Still active in timber rattlesnake hunt competitions, Rawley Grant of Galeton is logged in with eight wins at Morris and Cross Fork, including three first-place and three second-place awards for the longest snake.

"When I was a kid on the farm, every snake had to be dead; so we killed every snake we saw—rattlesnakes and everything else. They'd come into the yard, and Mother would kill 'em—with rakes and hoes. We'd shoot 'em with shotguns, .22's, whatever. That was when I was very young. When I got to be a teenager— the first rattlers I ever caught—I caught two one night. We were ridin' around and carrying on, you know; it was after dark. We were down near Leetonia and saw two of 'em in the road. I had one in each hand. They wouldn't let me bring 'em in the van, so I had to hold 'em out the window. We ended up down in Morris; we sold 'em down there to a guy that owned a bar. It seemed exciting, so we just caught 'em alive all the time after that and started enterin' the hunts. That was probly in the mid-sixties. The first time I won anything was 1974.

"One time I took one down to one of those hunts, down the

line, run by one of those reptile clubs. It was over forty-nine inches—it would have won that hunt. They dumped him out to measure him, and the guy took his hook there and ground its head right down into the dirt. Blood started comin' out; this guy says, 'This snake is injured.' So they disqualified me, and, naturally, one of their guys won with a smaller snake. They might have cleaned their act up a bit lately, but, years ago, they were a pretty rough bunch of people. I didn't care for 'em at all. Mike [Rachiele] saw it happen. They were a shady bunch of people. They claim to be professionals, yet they all have 'sunken fang' medals on their lapels—how many times they've been bitten. I don't consider that being professional, gettin' bit all the time.

"I went to take two big ones back to their den last year, but I couldn't get 'em right to the den. A coyote run me right out of the woods—scared me half to death. All's I had was my stick, and this thing is yippin', and howlin', and circlin' me. It kept comin' closer. I'd holler at it, and it would bark right back and just scream at me—must of had pups or somethin'. I was about two hundred yards out from the den, so I just dumped the snakes out and ran. I went back this year and never saw a snake at that den. I've seen as many as thirteen in that one before. I don't know if the coyote killed 'em or not.

"With the Fish Commission regulations, I don't know; maybe people, knowin' that the snakes are protected, won't skid the tires over 'em and stone 'em. But the dedicated snake hunter, he's gonna buy a permit and hunt. I don't know what impact a season will have on helping the snake population. All's it might do is put the fire companies, like Morris and Cross Fork, in jeopardy. What's more important, a fire company or a rattlesnake? This is a big fund raiser for the fire companies, you know. But is it worth jeopardizing a potentially threatened species? I don't know. It's hard to say.

"I never cared for 'em using the squeeze box for measuring snakes—I don't think they give an accurate measurement; but then I'm only thinkin' of myself gettin' a better measurement on a long snake. Probably it's better for the snake than havin' three guys pullin' on 'im, 'cause when you're hangin' on to that neck, that neck is pretty fragile. Can't do the snake much good when you're pullin' on 'im like that. But when they're under the plexiglas, they're all contracted, and you can't get an accurate measurement.

"The biggest timber rattler I ever saw was the one John Howe had down at Morris one year—it was just over fifty-five inches. You hear rumors about big snakes, but they're measured dead. You have to consider the source and the lack of knowledge of people. Most people exaggerate. But I think there's a sixty-incher out there.

"I don't ever remember a timber rattler striking at me on my first approach. It's not until you harass 'em a little bit—touch 'em—that they'll become aggressive. I've walked by 'em—eighteen inches—lookin' at another snake, and had no response out of 'em whatever.

"One time I was huntin' with my flatlander buddy, Bob Dennis, from Cleveland. I don't remember if Jimm [Leach] was with us or not. I didn't have high boots or leggin's, just low boots. There was a bunch of rattlers—eight of 'em—around this one rock. I was standin' on this rock—it was on a pretty steep angle—and I lost traction. I slid off the rock, and I landed right on top of a coiled one. The way I landed, there was only about two inches of his head and neck stickin' out, and he couldn't strike me. But he was tryin'. So I did a reverse high jump, and cleared the trees, I think, gettin' back on the rock. If he would've had eight, ten inches stickin' out, he'd of nailed me. I think the most exciting thing is when you're gettin' real close to a known den, and ya know there's snakes there, and ya trip in the laurel and fall down. You can get up real quick. There's nothin' like fallin' when ya know they're around—and there you are, layin' on the ground."

During the past thirty years, John Howe, of Nelson, established legendary status as the premier rattlesnake hunter of Tioga County. Be-

tween 1972 and 1977, he snatched the "Longest" award at Morris on five occasions and the "Most" three times; he still holds the hunt's all-time record for the biggest timber rattler—fifty-five and one-half inches.

"I was seventeen years old, trout fishing up Tim Ives Run. I almost stepped on a big rattler that lay on an old log road. I ran down the road—I was deathly afraid of rattlers. Then I stopped and picked up a long stick. I went back. I'd heard all kinds of rumors about how far they would strike and all that crap. I prodded him a little, then got a shorter stick. I decided to kill him and take him home to show my dad. I was carrying him down the path, and, when I got to the place I'd stopped when I was running from him, there was another one. So I knocked him in the head and took both snakes home.

"The following Saturday I went back out; you know, I said, 'This isn't that bad.' I went up behind the Middlebury Milk Plant. I was gone about an hour. When I came back, I had forty-one snakes. I mean there was nothin' but rattlesnakes up there— a lot of 'em got away. Two weeks later I decided I was gonna ketch one alive. I went back up in the hollow. I saw a big one tucked back in under a rock. I had a snare, you know, a stick with a loop. So I got the noose around his neck and got a good hold on 'im, all with good intentions of taking him alive. He got to turning and broke his neck. After that, I went out and bought a good catcher, a regular snake catcher. Then I didn't kill 'em anymore. That was back in the early sixties.

"I sold the snakes to a guy from Batavia, N.Y., and he'd sell 'em to a milk farm in Louisiana. They used 'em for the venom. I got ten dollars apiece. It was for a good cause, you know, the medical industry. I never turned 'em in for the bounty once I started ketchin' 'em alive. I don't know how many hundreds I sold—a lot—about nine hundred, one year alone. I caught 107 in one day. There were a lot of areas I hunted: Westfield to Mansfield, Middlebury, Trout Run, Monroeton—all over.

"I started entering at Morris in the mid-sixties. I went a few years before I won. Herold Jenkins was the one I was trying to beat—he was an old-time snake hunter; he won at Monroeton a lot, too. After I beat him, he saw to it that I got an invitation to the Monroeton Hunt. I went over and took all four trophies, 'Longest' and 'Most' for rattlesnakes and copperheads. The next year I took three of 'em, then I never went back. The Monroeton gang had figured that I didn't know that country, but I'd been over there berrying with friends from Canton. Farmers

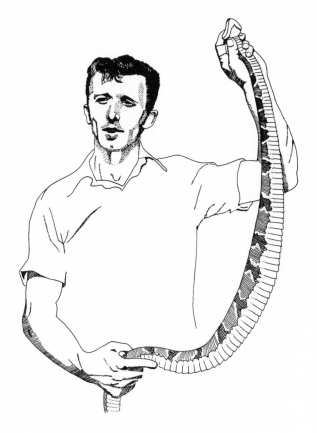

can tell you a lot, too; they're out there all the time workin' the ground, hayin' it, and mending fences. They see the rattlers, and they don't like 'em. They'll tell you all they can.

"I caught one up behind LaPoint's place; he measured sixty inches. That's the biggest timber rattler I've ever seen—he was bright yellow—the prettiest, brightest rattler. It was after the hunt, so I sold 'im. He was an old one. You take a person that's deathly afraid of snakes, they see a three-foot timber rattler and think it's six feet long.

"I only got bit once—a fang in the finger—way back when I first started huntin' 'em. I knew better even before I did it. I had fifteen snakes in the bag, and I wanted an even number, you know. I saw this one about forty inches long or so. He got goin' under this rock, and only a short section of his tail was stickin' out. So I said, 'I'll just grab it and give it a quick jerk,' but I knew I shouldn't. You know what they do, don't you? As soon as they go under, they bring their head right back around to guard the entrance. They're waiting for you. I knew they did that; I just thought I could get away with it if I were quick enough. Rattle-snakes are real quick. My arm swelled up for about a week. All the swelling and everything just stopped right here [armpit], and a sack formed. For some odd reason, all the poison gathered right here and formed kind of a bunch. Then it broke, and, after it drained, I was OK. Never went to the doctor. I never figured there was that much venom, you know—just one fang.

"I think it's a good idea to do what they did [the Fish Commission regulations]. The snakes were getting thinned out quite a bit in some areas. They could have exterminated them in some spots. Some areas got hammered steady. But there are other spots where nobody hunted them. And there's some places where there's so much rock that they'll never wipe 'em out—steep sides that are nothin' but rock piled five feet deep. To start with, in those places, you can't sneak up on 'em. They feel the vibrations of the sliding rocks as you're walkin'. Spots like that, there's always gonna be a lot of snakes.

"I quit entering hunts about eight years ago. I figured, 'I had my time; it's time to get out of it.' I take pictures now. I spend a lot of time in the woods. My boy told me, just today, that he'd like to win a trophy at Morris for the 'Longest.' He's gonna have to find it himself. I had to learn on my own. I spent a lot of time hunting, scouting; you don't do it overnight. I had sore feet every day, then I'd turn around and go the next day—over and over."

A renowned ex-bounty hunter, Gerald Ellis, from East Lawrence, has pursued timber rattlers for over forty years, relentlessly during the first thirty. As a teenager without a vehicle, he'd walk for miles just to get to rattler country. His awards from Morris include first places in the "Most," "Longest," and "Most Rattles" categories. As long as this man is walking, he'll be searching for timbers.

"I've hunted 'em ever since I was twelve or thirteen. My dad and I used to go up in the ledges and get 'em for the oil. We used to take the fat and render it down—use it for earache medicine. We used to keep the rattles in a match box. That's when I first got into it. When they came out with the bounty, why, I got into it for bounty. Every year that they ever paid the bounty, except three, I hunted for bounty—I think they paid it for twenty-seven years. I was in the service those three years. I was in it from the beginning. I turned as high as five hundred a year in for bounty.

"It was more profitable late in the summer. Say ya walk into the den in June and see five or six big ones—five or six bucks; ya wait 'til September and ya might get a hundred—open the snakes right up and take the young ones out. Sure, I done that lots of times. There's a trick to everything. If you're gonna hunt 'em for bounty, there hain't no use in walkin' in and gettin' five dollars when ya can walk in and get a hundred. You know, they wanted the snakes killed; that's what we done. I used to give my wife, Pat, the money for the kids for school clothes. I turned the tails in at the bounty agent's—there was a fellow in Holiday, one in Morris, and one in Wellsboro. We used to have some trouble with 'em over the small snakes. They didn't wanna pay on 'em; so, then we'd take 'em over to the commissioners—take 'em right over and put 'em on their desk. They paid. They told us to take 'em right back over to the agent and get our money.

"I think a lot of the trouble with the population of the snakes is everything gettin' built up so much anymore—camps and everything. The snakes are movin' back just as far as they can move. And what snakes are around them camps, people are killin' 'em. We had a ledge over in Knoxville. The first time we went over there, we got nine in the field and a bunch of 'em up on the ledge. After that it was always good for three or four. They put a camp up in there, and there ain't been a snake since. I'll bet them guys go up in there and shoot the devil out of 'em. I don't care what the Fish Commission does; people are still gonna knock 'em in the head. People's still afraid of 'em. Nine out of ten people, when they see 'em, try to run over 'em or knock 'em in the head.

"There's snakes. Certain areas, you know, they'll always be snakes; but certain areas there's not gonna be any either. I got areas I cleaned out entirely when I was huntin' for bounty. There's not a snake in 'em. You go up Mitchell Crick—Charlie Button lives up there. He can tell you there's not a snake back of his place. Then down below him by the chicken farm—they used to be there; there's no snakes there anymore. Then back above Charlie's, on the left, where the old Baker farm used to be—there's no snakes there anymore. I cleaned 'em out of all three places. I mean they're gone—entirely. There ain't even one snake in there.

"I don't do that anymore. I put 'em back. So do some of the other guys, like Burdette [Brewer]. That's just a few of us that does that. There's still guys out there that are gonna pound the devil out of 'em when they run into 'em. Some guys don't put 'em back where they find 'em, too. They just take 'em out and dump 'em, and the snakes just keep goin'. May never see 'em again—may never make it. They're disoriented. John [Howe] and I dumped forty-six big ones right out on one rock in a good spot we'd about cleaned out. We never found a one of 'em after that. They go here and there—easy pickin's; the hawks get em; the deer stomp 'em.

"I don't know what this season they're talkin' about is gonna do for 'em. They're concerned about protectin' the pregnant females. You can find them pregnant snakes layin' 'round the den all summer; I don't know what the season's gonna do for 'em. They're talkin' about chargin' more for permits, too; I don't know if they figure that's gonna discourage fellas from huntin' or not. I think they just had a little extra money to spend when they went into this checkin' 'em out and taggin' 'em and everything—wanted to give somebody a job for a while. They can have all the permits and studies they want, but ya can't protect 'em. That's all there is to it, unless they put somebody out there to pinch these people that are knockin' 'em in the head. People will always kill 'em. They're afraid of 'em.

"John and I got together and were huntin' over in Bear Crick, one day. We propped up a nice slab of shalerock in a field, and John said, 'In a year or so we'll come back and find a nice one.' I went back the next year and got the nice one. John said, 'Darn ya, ya just couldn't wait.' I said, 'Nope, I couldn't think of any place to find a big one, so I just went back, and there he was.' He was fifty-four inches. That was '76, and I haven't got another snake out of there since.

"John and I were here one day; we each had a box of rattlers sittin' here by the trailer. A couple college kids stopped—they wanted to look at our snakes. So we opened a box up, and this big one came right over the top and went right in under my trailer. John went right under on his hands and knees and grabbed 'im by the tail and brought 'im back out. Those college boys, they got right in the car and left. They said, 'You guys are crazy.' John would walk 'em right around by the tail. Yeah, he'd hunt day and night. Heck, he'd hunt 'em in Horton Hollow when it was gettin' so dark he'd have to light a match to pick the last one up. Yeah, he could hear 'im and everything—didn't know where he was; lit a match and there he was, lookin' right at 'im. Picked 'im up with the catcher and put 'im in the bag. We're talkin' a short bag, a pillowcase—and he already had eight big ones in it. He had to stuff that one in. They didn't wanna stay in; he'd cuff 'em and make 'em stay in anyway. Yeah, he'd steal a pillowcase right off his wife's pillow, and away he'd go."

If there's something going on involving timber rattlers in northeastern Tioga County, chances are Burdette Brewer knows about it. When area schools, parks, or organizations are looking for a good rattler program, they call Burdette. And he always has a snake or two on hand to show visitors at his hilltop farm near Lawrenceville. He's hunted rattlers in seven other states, participating in the Sweetwater Texas Hunt "when they caught ten tons of diamondbacks"; but Burdette just loves to talk timber rattler.

"My brother and I went down to the Morris Snake Hunt in 1970. At that time there were no regulations on snakes and they'd get all they wanted. My lands! We couldn't believe it—they'd be bringin' in snakes by the boxes and bags full! That got to botherin' us, because my brother and I lived the mountains—spent a lot of time in the mountains; we never dreamed there were any rattlers in our mountains—we never saw any. So suspicion finally got the best of us; we got ahold of a snake hunter down there. His name was Herold Jenkins. He volunteered to take us over to Barclay—he had a camp over there. So my brother and I went over there a couple of times, but we didn't get there early enough—Herold beat us out. We finally got around in time to catch him. Herold was good, very good. He told us all about the snakes, and he showed us how to handle the snakes.

"After a couple years, we got brave enough to go ourselves. It's a fantastic hobby! It is! Really! I mean—there's a lot to it!

One of the things I really enjoy is getting out there in the mountains and seein' the dogwoods in blossom. You see flowers there in May that people never see. How about the laurel! I mean most people don't see such beautiful laurel. Sure they see a little along the roads here and there—nothin' like the blankets you see in the wild. We just enjoy it tremendously. The rattlers fascinate me. They're an interesting little critter—that's just what they are.

"After we started huntin' 'em, I don't think we went back to the Morris Hunt more than once or twice. We would rather go huntin' 'em on our own. We never participated in any of the competitions like they have at some of the hunts—you know— the sacking contests and such; I was always a little opposed to that. I'm glad they never did that down here at Morris. I don't think that's fair to the snake. We feel that the snake has a place in the wild. If we bring snakes in for a display or program, we take them back to their home dens so they survive. I don't want to see them eliminated. I think that if the snake hunting had continued unregulated, we wouldn't have any rattlers today. Shortly after we got to huntin' them, it got pretty hard to find snakes—awful hard. And they haven't really rebounded. It takes a long time for 'em to replenish. I always thought we could find an area where nobody had been and find fifteen or twenty, but we never have—they're just hunted too much. I disapprove of guys tippin' rocks when they're huntin' snakes. I know guys that just tear the dens apart. That's not right—it's just not right. Sure they find snakes. That's not my kind of huntin'. Once in a while I'll tip one up, but I'll put it right back in its original position. When I go back, I'll find a snake. Those guys won't. You must leave the snakes' habitat just as it is.

"If you told me you saw a six-foot timber rattler here in Tioga County, I wouldn't call you a liar to your face—but that's impossible, just impossible. The average snake here is thirty-five to forty-five inches. If we get a fifty- or fifty-two-inch snake, why, we got a big snake. Anything over that is rare. We're always lookin' for the big one—there's snakes out there that'll go sixty, live measure.

"I was bitten because of my carelessness. I usually wear high lineman's boots; but last June, that day, I knew we had a long hike. I looked at them boots, and my feet got to hurtin', just lookin' at 'em. So I figured I'd be safe with my regular work boots—the fellow I was huntin' with was wearin' sneakers [Gerald Ellis]. See, I'm not used to huntin' with these low boots on; and when I caught this snake—about a forty-incher—I had ahold of him a little too far back toward the tail. I was backin' up through some rocks and brush, tryin' to get him in the open. He got his fang—just one fang—in a vein in my leg; how I don't know; it was done in the snap of a finger. As soon as it happened, I began to feel burning, see. I knew I'd been bit. I'd read up on snakebite; I knew what to expect. We got the snake in the bag, and my partner said, 'Let's go to the hospital.' I said, 'Wait 'til I check out this other nice rock over here.' So I went over there and bagged a nice yellow one. By that time—about three minutes—my throat and my tongue were tingling. We headed in to the hospital.

My bite was different. Usually the venom destroys the muscle and tissue and causes blackness and swelling almost immediately. Not mine. The doctor cleaned up my leg. I was tingling all over by then—you know what it's like when your arm goes to sleep—my whole body was tingling like that. The doctor said, 'I don't think you got any venom at all'—none! I said, 'Doc, I tingle all over.' He said, 'Listen, if I'd been bit by a snake, I'd be tinglin' too.' So he sent me home! When I got home, my leg was startin' to swell and was burnin' so bad I could hardly stand on it. My daughter and my son-in-law are both nurses. They came down and checked me out and got me right back to the hospital. Another doctor checked me—one with snakebite experience. He said, 'I don't think you got bit.' At the same time, a nurse was shaking a bottle of blood that she had drawn out of my arm. She kept shakin' it and shakin' it. I looked at her and says, 'Are you having a problem?' She said, 'Well it just isn't coagulating like it should.' I says, 'You know why? Full of rattlesnake venom— that's why!'

I was in there four days. The venom destroyed the platelets. The normal count should be 150,000 to 450,000. My platelets had dropped down to 3,000—3,000! They said if I would have had an ulcer or something, I would've bled to death. They made some phone calls, then started pumping me full of platelets and antivenin. I don't know how many of those vials they put into me. They kept 'em flowin' until the count came up and stayed up.

"The rattlesnake is part of our nation. We don't want it to become extinct. Like the eagle, we have to preserve it. The rattlesnake has its place—let's leave it there. The timber rattlesnake isn't endangering man's life in any way whatsoever. A rattlesnake never goes and chases a man; he'll never bite you unless you're tormentin' him in some way. I think it's fantastic we have a law out there to help protect them."

12

Losing the Battle

❚❚ **S**TONEWALL"—THAT WAS THE NAME I GAVE TO the lunker I picked up where the top of the fields meet the big woods down on Lycoming Creek.

In June 1992, my old partner, Gary Dillman, made a trek back to a favorite den we'd discovered during the early eighties. It was a den we could count on for twelve to fifteen sightings— we'd never taken a snake there or turned a rock. On his way up the right side of the hollow, he glimpsed a crew of guys coming down the other side—and they appeared to be carrying snake sticks. When Gary reached the denning area, he discovered that it had been shredded. The rocks were flipped and the snakes were gone. It was disheartening news, considering my concern for the future of *C. horridus;* but it was only the beginning of a "bad news summer."

Around midsummer an acquaintance told me he'd acquired an amateur video of a timber rattlesnake hunt. I went over to take a look, already knowing what to expect, but hoping that our new generation of snake hunters had matured—fat chance! I was a bit dismayed upon seeing the only rattler captured by the "star" of the film lash out as he ran at it with his outstretched pincers. (I'd never seen that in twenty years of hunting timbers.) The video went on to show just how "mean" the serpents are. With his thick leather boots, the hunter would step on the snake, several inches behind its head. Naturally, the snake would turn and frantically bite at the boot. Using the pincers, the hunter would grab the snake by the neck, then drag it around for a while to show "proper" handling techniques.

On my way home, I kept running the strike episode over and over in my mind—I'm not known to have quick wit, and I'm a bit slow to recognize an illusion. I was six miles down the highway before realizing why the rattler had acted abnormally. It was the slight blip in the video that gave it away: timber rattlesnakes don't lie around basking in a defensive coil configuration; they use the resting coil—if they *are* coiled—from which a strike like the one taped cannot be executed. The hunter first grabbed the basking snake, then he moved it away from its escape crevice, forcing it into a defensive coil: "Lights, camera, action!"

But Stonewall—well, I don't normally get so attached to an individual critter. It all started on an unsettled mid-July evening—cool, occasional light showers broken by bright, warm rays of sunshine, a rainbow evening. I pulled into the driveway of the abandoned farm, grabbed my gear, and headed up the steep hill, through the tall, wet grass. I had a forty-six-inch male black rattler that I'd used for a program that day; I wanted to release him at the outcropping where I'd captured him, about a mile back on top.

I maintained a hurried pace, anticipating a little hunting if the sun was cooperative after making the release. Finally, I reached the sandstone boulders that my rattler had been using as his shedding headquarters. After watching him disappear into his crevice, I began meandering around the ridge top, hoping to spot another snake or two. But soon I gave up—it was too cool and damp to waste time hunting the mountaintop. I dropped off the ridge, breaking out of the woods on the steep, sunny side at the top of the old grass field. Now, steady sunshine was burning off the few remaining wisps of mist—I removed my flannel shirt. I surveyed the big field, looking for rock of any kind, then headed for a manmade stone pile where a fencerow intersected the woods about 150 yards to my right.

When I was twenty yards from the rocks, I stopped to make a

detailed inspection. I spotted a rattler sprawled across the small stones near the center of the heap—it was trying to soak in a little warmth before nightfall. I walked slowly and steadily, directly toward the snake; I was ready to dash if it gave the slightest indication of running. But old Stonewall was hurtin' for sunshine—he wasn't about to run. He slowly slipped into a defensive coil only when I'd cut the distance to about six feet. He was a big one. "I have to take him in to show Donna and the kids," I thought. "I'll be gentle with him and let him go in a day or two."

While I hung my bag in a small tree, Stonewall just sat there watching me, whirling his stub of a rattle—he'd lost most of the heavy string. I reached with my stick, ever so slowly, gently sliding the open steel loop beneath his midsection without drawing a strike—I didn't want Stonewall's ordeal to commence with a broken fang. He held the coil, allowing me to drop him into the cloth sack with ease.

Stonewall was an impressive black-patterned timber rattlesnake. He'd probably been born a dozen or more years prior, about the time Tioga County dropped the bounty on his kind. He measured fifty inches as he lay on the garage floor, snugging himself against the wall. His midsection was the diameter of a coffee-shop mug. His every move was calculated to elude his captor—without lowering his guard.

Two days later I carried Stonewall back to his summer pad. He eased out of the bag, raised his head high, then glided across the stone pile and into the tall grass. I reassured myself as I trudged back to my vehicle: he knows where he's at; he'll calm down and come back—there's a reason he's made it this long. Two weeks later Stonewall was dead, hacked to pieces by a man shoveling out a spring seep near his cabin, which was a few hundred yards below the rock pile. Yeah, rattlesnake news travels quickly in the Northern Tier: "a fifty-four-incher" was "going after the man"; "only had three rattles 'cause he threw

the rest of 'em during the fight." Nonsense! I knew Stonewall—
personally!

I threw Stonewall out of sync. He'd made it for a dozen,
maybe twenty years or more; then I came along to bend a cog.

13

Endangered?

N *PIONEER LIFE; OR, THIRTY YEARS A HUNTER,* **PHILIP** Tome describes, among other things, a Northcentral Pennsylvania pioneer's encounters with timber rattlesnakes. The Tomes were among a handful of settlers sprinkled throughout the Pine Creek Valley in 1795. Tome's report on rattlesnakes is quite interesting. In his day, accurate knowledge of snakes being limited, old wives' tales were accepted as scientific gospel by many. (Rattlesnake legends are so persistent that many otherwise educated individuals of our own day continue the tradition: "they don't die 'til the sun goes down"; "they always rattle before they strike"; "they swallow their young to protect them.") Yet Tome, in repeating some of the tales, made it clear that he had not personally observed such behavior.

Tome was aware that color phase did not reveal the rattler's sex, and he knew that more than one rattle segment could be added each year. He reported that rattlesnakes were so plentiful in some sections that travelers would spend the nights in their canoes, anchored in midstream. He quizzed Cornplanter, who was quite familiar with Pine Creek's rattlesnake reputation, about dealing with the serpents. The Indian chief told of wearing leggings and fabricating sleeping platforms when spending time in rattler infested territory. He also explained that burning the woods in May was a tactic to rid the area of snakes.

Early settlers also burned the woods to clear them cf rattlesnakes—in the long run, they were creating better rattler habitat—but the "big burn" occurred during the peak of the lumbering era. Between 1870 and 1920 timbering and wide-spread forest fires virtually eliminated the upper forest canopy in Northcentral Pennsylvania. In one two-week period, May 6–20, 1891, it seems as though all of Tioga County was ablaze, according to accounts in the *Wellsboro Agitator*. Individual articles describe large fires burning at Bloss Mountain, Maple Hill, Landrus, Long Run, Stony Fork, Pine Creek, Leetonia, Kettle Creek, Westfield, Brookfield, Middlebury, Baldwin Run, and Marsh Creek. Sawmills, barns, homes, and piled logs were destroyed. In some communities, townspeople dug pits in their yards to bury household goods in an effort to protect them from the advancing conflagration. "Fires burning M. L. Harrison's tract on the East Rim caused a roar that could be heard a mile away. Flames shot two hundred feet into the air and green trees were falling like so many straws" (May 20). Local news from Painter Run: "We didn't have any Sunday the 10th, there was so much fire" (May 20).

As a result of these fires, and those that occurred throughout the early 1900s, vast acreages of rock outcroppings and slides, previously shaded by mature timber, were exposed to sunlight. A lush growth of grasses, ferns, brambles, huckleberries, and other vegetation favorable to small mammals and birds ensued. The Black Forest became prime breeding grounds for timber rattlesnakes. Rattlesnake encounters in communities nestled in the mountains escalated; reports of denning areas containing hundreds of rattlers were common. Some typical headlines in the *Wellsboro Agitator:*

• July 21, 1909: "Boy Bitten by Big Rattlesnake" (twice in the knee, expected to recover)

• September 1, 1909: "Boy Falls on Rattlesnake" (didn't bite him, but scared him so badly that he was ill for a few days)

• July 20, 1910: "Man Dies from Effects of Rattlesnake Bite" (was berrying on Cobble Hill, poked at snake with stick, was struck in thumb, died sixteen hours later due to "paralyzed heart")

• July 20, 1910: "Ranger Kills Season's Largest Rattler" (Samuel Lebo, Lucullus, five-foot snake)

• August 10, 1910: "Cat Kills Rattlesnake" (cat fools snake by pretending to be hypnotized, then pounces in for kill, Barclay area)

• June 28, 1911: "A Tall Snake Story from Bradford County" (ate two rabbits, fell into a hole, couldn't get out, threw rattles at a railroad worker to get his attention)

• July 5, 1911: "Another Snake Story" (Center County fisherman bothered by numerous snakes driven to stream by forest fire)

And some typical articles:

Rattlesnakes on Pine Creek

There are some thrilling incidents recorded of encounters with rattlesnakes in the Pine Creek gorge this season. The other morning as the Central train drew up at Ross, between Slate Run and Cammal, for the passenger train to pass, a brakeman stooped to open a switch. He had his hand on the ground when he felt something brush by his shoe. Dropping the switch lever, he turned and saw a yellow and black snake glide between his legs and down the railroad embankment.

The brakeman picked up a club and soon killed the reptile. It was a rattler, four feet long and adorned with five bells. It had been "asleep at the switch" and when the brakeman awoke it, it had glided by his hand, and not many inches from his face.

Other New York Central men say that rattlesnakes were never so abundant as they are on Pine Creek this year. On the mountain about Blackwell, huckleberry pickers have abandoned their trips on account of the prevalence of the poisonous snakes. A civil engineer on a forest preserve in Tioga County has killed 27 rattlers on his tramps over the mountain thus far this summer. Last week was his record week, as the hot summer is bringing the rattlers down to seek the watering places.

Railroad men say it is dangerous to walk along the tracks in snake country. Rattlers seek the hot rails and beds of the railroad to hide and sun themselves. They crawl up under the flange of the rails, and the innocent track walker or section hand does not know of his danger until he steps on the snake or gets within reach of the poisonous fangs. (August 10, 1910)

A Tough Rattlesnake

Last Friday Lyman Mitchell, of Tioga township, stepped out of his rig just below the W. L. Button place to kill a rattlesnake, when his horse took fright and ran away. Mrs. Button saw the horse coming and ran out and stopped the animal.

When Mr. Mitchell came along to get his horse he told Mrs. Button that he had stopped to kill a snake, but didn't have time to do it. She then went down the road armed with a club, found the snake and pounded it until it should have been dead, but it wasn't. Mrs. Button thought she had finished it; however, cut off its rattles and hung the snake over a wire fence.

Mr. Button and Harry Wheeler went to look at the snake that evening, but it was not on the fence. When they returned home Mrs. Button exhibited the 13 rattles as proof of her exploit.

The next morning, as Mr. Button was passing the place where Mrs. Button had fought the rattler, he saw the same snake ready for battle, and to make a thorough job of it he cut off its head. Later in the day Mr. Button killed another rattlesnake, which "sported" nine rattles. (June 14, 1911)

As the rattlesnake population exploded, community leaders, woodsmen, miners, and other residents joined forces in an attempt to eliminate the nuisance. Jacks, levers, draft teams, dynamite, guns, and clubs were deployed to the rocky slopes;

bounties were established. The natural thing to do was to kill the snakes.

When the logging interests moved on, the commonwealth's forest acquisition program was in full swing. More environmentally sound logging practices were established, and a forest fire protection organization was developed. The forest regenerated naturally with fast-growing hardwoods. As the canopy closed, the rattler brooding areas began to shrink accordingly. The Department of Forests and Waters and the Civilian Conservation Corps established a system of roads throughout the state forest, opening the door to increased recreational use. Permanent campsite leases were granted in an additional effort to make the newly acquired lands available to the public. These developments further encroached upon the timber rattler's grounds.

With snake populations still high well into the fifties and sixties, annual organized rattlesnake roundups began to appear throughout Northcentral Pennsylvania. The sponsor could raise money, reduce the snake population, and entertain the public. At the time, thinning the rattlesnake population was an invigorating, wholesome, and beneficial outdoor sport; a wide range of people participated. There was also a market for live rattlers, and some locals hunted for profit throughout the summers. Buyers marketed the serpents for food, zoo subjects, and novelty items. Other hunters chose to kill the snakes, preferably just prior to birthing time. The mother's and extracted young's tails brought one dollar each at the local bounty headquarters. It was easier and more profitable to carry ten dollar's worth of tails off the mountain as opposed to lugging out a live adult snake worth the same, at most.

As the timber rattlesnake population dwindled, the annual roundups continued, more as a fundraising and sporting event than a needed function to protect the populace. Hunters had to work harder, traveling into remote areas to locate the remaining active dens. The number of hunters returning empty-handed at day's end was on the rise. The effects of handling, displacing, and killing of rattlesnakes, combined with the damaging of dens and the naturally shrinking acreage of quality brooding grounds, reduced the timber rattlesnake population to, perhaps, an all-time low in Northcentral Pennsylvania—and it has already been eliminated from much of its historical national range.

The lack of basking sites concentrates the remaining snakes into fewer and smaller sunny openings where they are more vulnerable to predators and snake hunters. Moreover, a drastic increase in the Northcentral wild turkey population occurred during the period of the timber rattler's equally dramatic decline. Some locals, including Ralph Miller of Morris, believe those big birds, known to kill infant rattlers, played a major role in the snake's decline. (At his general store in Morris, Ralph served as a rattlesnake bounty agent for Tioga County. He is an experienced snake hunter.)

Today, active dens are few and far between. An hour's travel through dense laurel and across rough terrain to one's favorite rattler den often results in disappointment. One might find that the rocks have been flipped, slid, and generally displaced; a shrub, once guarding the snakes' favorite crevice, has been uprooted and lies withered nearby; an empty cigarette pack and several spent cartridges are scattered about. There are no rattlers.

Wildlife biologists believe that when populations of some species like the slow-moving, short-ranging timber rattlesnake are reduced dramatically, the inability to find mates will deliver a sudden and final blow. Are we nearing that fine line? Twenty years ago, most any Northcentral forestry road crew was accustomed to seeing a dozen rattlers during the grading season. The going rate today is a snake or two.

Perhaps it's not too late for *Crotalus horridus* here in Northcentral Pennsylvania, one of its last remaining strongholds. Bounties have been withdrawn. The Pennsylvania Fish and Boat Commission has established regulations pertaining to permits, seasons, bag limits, capture methods, and destruction of dens.

Although enforcement is marginal in our age of budget crunches, true sportsmen and outdoor enthusiasts will study and honor the regulations. Positive information and education may be the deciding factor. Maybe I'm naive in believing we can alter people's hatred for this New World snake. Changing public opinion on this issue may be comparable to convincing a Yuppie to install sixty-watt light bulbs. Yesterday, I listened to a nationally broadcast radio commentator describe some celebrity's encounter with a "vicious" timber rattler; the snake's skin now decorates a golf club. I looked up *rattlesnake* in a thesaurus; it's listed under "evil-doer" along with "pyromaniac, terrorist, desperado, cannibal, and fiend."

My belief in habitat improvement as a way to ensure the future of the timber rattler may finally convince certain people that I am insane. Those who've accompanied me on midsummer tree girdling missions (to create or expand basking areas) will surely testify in their favor. When I suggest that the gypsy moth was sent to save the rattlesnakes, eyebrows rise. I do hope that conservation agencies monitoring the plight of the timber rattlesnake will make the required adjustments, as necessary, to assure its survival.

The circle of snake hunters I mix with has evolved into a group of rattlesnake observers. We see how many snakes we can find, try to locate new den sites, and check old dens to determine what kind of changes are taking place. The last time I was party to bringing a rattler home with intentions to kill it was four years ago. My daughter, Tushanna, had located and captured a large yellow phase. I told her it wouldn't hurt to take one snake, suggesting that we'd make a rattlesnake casserole and mount the skin. When we arrived home we reversed our decision upon receiving a severe tongue-lashing (which was also a well-construed lecture) from Tushanna's mother (and, of course, my wife). All the preaching I'd done about saving the rattlers had apparently hit home. Shanny and I grabbed the bag of snake, retreated to the Bronco, and headed for the wilds to release the catch.

Shanny has become equally hard-nosed about snake killers. A couple of summers ago, while on an "observing mission," we crossed paths with a couple of her male schoolmates who were bumming around with their .22 rifles. We had just left a denning area, having spotted six rattlers; we didn't let on what we were doing. The young men told us to be careful because there were rattlesnakes in the area. One of them pointed up the trail and said, "Just last summer we found two of 'em right there." I held my breath to no avail as, in an astonishing display of the existence of the human aura, I saw Shanny glow as she formulated

the retaliation to the answer she knew she would receive to a question she was about to ask.

Tushanna asked, "What did you do then?" I took a step back. "We killed 'em," the one young fellow replied. There is a saying that "hell hath no fury like a woman scorned." Shanny may have been just exasperated, not scorned, but those kids sure didn't know the difference.

If anyone implies that it took courage to handle or kill a "nasty old rattler," I hope you will realize the truth of the matter: that person is misinformed and excessively scared of the animal; or, as in the case of the dime-a-dozen, snake-killer exhibitionist, a braggart and a liar.

I do not suggest we allow timber rattlers to frequent our neighborhoods. People should not be expected to suffer a snakebite while playing or working in their community. I would be the first to support reduction of the nearest rattler colony if a community had more than occasional encounters with timber rattlesnakes. If the areawide snake population boomed, and regulations were eased, I'd be willing to join in the harvest. I believe that renewable resources such as forests and wild game should be properly harvested and utilized in accordance to their respective management plans. However, considering the current status of the timber rattlesnake, the title "Environmental Criminal" befits anyone who travels deep into the forest and kills such a magnificent animal with the idea that he or she is helping civilization.

If you're ever near the upper ledges on a sunny June afternoon, feel the warmth of the sandstone boulders; savor the aroma of laurel blossoms and sweet fern; receive the whisper of the distant tumbling brook; study the raptors soaring below; then, carefully weave your way among the ledges—an awesome sight awaits.

References

Subject Index

Name Index

REFERENCES

Appleby, Leonard G. 1980. "Snakes Shedding Skin." *Natural History* 89 (February): 64–71.

Brown, William S. 1993. *Biology, Status, and Management of the Timber Rattlesnake (Crotalus horridus): A Guide for Conservation.* Herpetological Circular No. 22. Society for the Study of Reptiles and Amphibians.

Galligan, J. H., and W. A. Dunson. 1979. "Biology and Status of Timber Rattlesnake Populations in Pennsylvania." *Biological Conservation* 15: 13–58.

Gamow, R. Igor, and John F. Harris. 1973. "The Infrared Receptors of Snakes." *Scientific American* 228 (13): 94–100.

Gans, Carl. 1970. "How Snakes Move." *Scientific American* 222 (6): 82–96.

Glaeser, Douglas J. 1969. *Geology of Flagstones in the Endless Mountains Region, Northern Pennsylvania.* Information Circular 66. Pennsylvania Bureau of Topographic and Geologic Survey.

Greene, Harry W. 1990. "A Sound Defense of the Rattlesnake." *Pacific Discovery* 43 (4): 10–19.

Klauber, Laurence M. 1972. *Rattlesnakes.* 2 vols. Berkeley and Los Angeles: University of California Press.

Mader, Douglas R. 1994. "Mouth Rot." *Reptiles* 1 (3): 24–27.

Martin, William H. 1988. "Life History of the Timber Rattlesnake." *Catesbeiana* 8 (March): 9–12.

———. 1992. "Phenology of the Timber Rattlesnake (*Crotalus horridus*) in an Unglaciated Section of the Appalachian Mountains." Pp. 259–77 in *The Biology of Pitvipers,* edited by J. A. Campbell and E. D. Brodie, Jr. Tyler, Texas: Selva Press.

Martin, William H., and W. H. Smith. 1990. "Distribution and Status of the Timber Rattlesnake in Pennsylvania." Report to the Carnegie Museum of Natural History and the Pennsylvania Fish Commission.

Puskar, Allan M. 1990. "The Timber Rattlesnake." *Newsletter of the League of Florida Herpetological Societies.* July.

Reinert, Howard K. 1984a. "Habitat Separation Between Sympatric Snake Populations." *Ecology* 65 (2): 478–86.

————. 1984b. "Habitat Variation Within Sympatric Snake Populations." *Ecology* 65 (5): 1673–82.

————. 1990. "A Profile and Impact Assessment of Organized Rattlesnake Hunts in Pennsylvania." *Journal of the Pennsylvania Academy of Science* 64 (3): 136–44.

————. 1991. "Translocation as a Conservation Strategy for Amphibians
and Reptiles: Some Comments, Concerns, and Observations."
Herpetologica 47 (3): 357–63.

————. 1992. "Radiotelemetric Field Studies of Pitvipers: Data Acquisition and Analysis." Pp. 185–97 in *The Biology of Pitvipers,* edited
by J. A. Campbell and E. D. Brodie, Jr. Tyler, Texas: Selva
Press.

————, and David Cundall. 1982. "An Improved Surgical Implantation
Method for Radio-Tracking Snakes." *Copeia* (3): 702–05.

————, with David Cundall and Lauretta M. Bushar. 1984. "Foraging
Behavior of the Timber Rattlesnake." *Copeia* (4): 976–81.

————, and Robert T. Zappalorti. 1988. "Timber Rattlesnakes (*Crotalus
horridus*) of the Pine Barrens: Their Movement Patterns and
Habitat Preference." *Copeia* (4): 964–78.

Shiffer, Clark. 1987. "The Timber Rattlesnake." *Pennsylvania Angler* 56
(October): 24–25.

Tome, Philip. 1854. *Pioneer Life; or, Thirty Years a Hunter* 1989 reprint of
the 1928 edition. Baltimore: Gateway Press.

Wright, A. H., and Anna A. Wright. 1957. *Handbook of Snakes* Vol. 2.
Ithaca, N.Y.: Comstock.

Zulich, Alan. 1992. "Snake Sex Determination by Probing." *Reptile and
Amphibian Magazine* (May-June): 21–23.

SUBJECT INDEX

NAME INDEX

PITT SERIES IN
NATURE AND NATURAL HISTORY

Marcia Bonta, Editor

Amphibians and Reptiles in West Virginia
N. Bayard Green and Thomas K. Pauley

Appalachian Autumn
Marcia Bonta

Appalachian Spring
Marcia Bonta

Atlas of Breeding Birds in Pennsylvania
Daniel W. Brauning, Editor

Buck Fever: The Deer Hunting Tradition in Pennsylvania
Mike Sajna

Guide to the Mammals of Pennsylvania
Joseph F. Merritt

Rattler Tales from Northcentral Pennsylvania
C. E. Brennan

Soldiers Delight Journal: Exploring a Globally Rare Ecosystem
Jack Wennerstrom

The West Virginia Breeding Bird Atlas
Albert R. Buckelew, Jr., and George A. Hall

Youghiogheny: Appalachian River
Tim Palmer